Escape from the French

Escape from the French

A Young Royal Navy Midshipman's Adventures During the Napoleonic War

Edward Boys

Escape from the French:
A *Young Royal Navy Midshipman's Adventures During the Napoleonic War*
by Edward Boys

First published under the title
Narrative of a Captivity and Adventures in France and Flanders Between the Years 1803 and 1809

Leonaur is an imprint
of Oakpast Ltd

Copyright in this form © 2009 Oakpast Ltd

ISBN: 978-1-84677-646-5 (hardcover)
ISBN: 978-1-84677-645-8 (softcover)

http://www.leonaur.com

Publisher's Notes

In the interests of authenticity, the spellings, grammar and place names used have been retained from the original editions.

The opinions of the authors represent a view of events in which he was a participant related from his own perspective, as such the text is relevant as an historical document.

The views expressed in this book are not necessarily those of the publisher.

Contents

Preface 9
Narrative 11
Appendix 144

To Rear-Admiral
Sir Edward W. C. R. Owen, K.C.B., M.P.
Surveyor-General of the Ordnance,
&c., &c., &c.

This Little Volume Containing a Plain and
Unpretending Narrative of Facts,
as a Tribute of High Esteem,
and Sincere Regard,
is Respectfully Inscribed,
by His Obliged Friend and Servant,
the Author.

Preface

The following *Narrative* was written in the West Indies, in 1810, at the previous suggestion, and for the sole amusement of my own family. With the view of leaving my children a memento of their father's juvenile adventures, I have since revised it, and formed the idea of committing it to the press, should more competent judges not deem such a course presumptuous.

The reader of this little volume can scarcely help observing that it could not have been published at the time it was written, without endangering those from whom I had received protection. When the lapse of years had removed this objection to its publication, I was restrained by the apprehension that it might be unworthy of general perusal; but, at length, trusting to the indulgence so generally shewn to naval authors, and more especially to the liberality of my brother officers, I venture, though still with diffidence, to publish this plain statement "of facts," requesting the candid reader to bear in mind, that I make no pretensions to literary merit, my sole object being to convey the simple truth in its simplest form.

Edward Boys

Narrative

At the termination of the war in the spring of 1802, I was paid off as a master's mate of the *Royal Sovereign*, bearing the flag of Vice-Admiral Sir Henry Harvey, K. B. In June following, I joined the *Phoebe* frigate; in September, Captain the Hon. T. B. Capel was appointed; we were sent to the Mediterranean, and there continued until the renewal of the war in 1803.

In July, the *Phoebe* was ordered off Toulon, to watch the enemy in that port: on our way thither, when off Civita Vecchia, two privateers were seen from the mast head, it being then a dead calm; the boats, ably manned and well armed, were dispatched in chase, under the orders of the first lieutenant, Perkins, and after five hours' rowing, about ten p. m. came up with one of them; but from an unfortunate medley of disastrous events, we were twice repulsed with the loss of eight men killed and wounded.

Having reached our station off Toulon, on the night of the 31st of July, two armed boats under the orders of Lieutenant Tickell, with one of which I was entrusted, were sent in shore for the purpose of capturing any vessel running along the coast, that he might judge worth the risk of attack; having gained an eligible situation, under the land, near Cape Cecie, we lay upon our oars until dawn of day, when two *settées* were discovered standing to the westward, with a light breeze; they were instantly boarded, and carried, without resistance; they proved to be from Genoa, bound to Marseilles, with fruit and sundry merchandise.

On rejoining the *Phoebe*, the sails of the prizes were found to be in such a tattered state, that Captain Capel judged it proper to detain them two days in order to have them repaired. I was then appointed prize-master to one, and a midshipman named Murray to the other, having with him an assistant brother officer, Whitehurst, whose name will frequently appear throughout this narrative.

Our orders were to proceed the following day to Lord Nelson, then off the coast of Catalonia, and thence to Malta. Unhappily for me it was otherwise ordained; for at break of day on the 4th of August, four French frigates, *viz. La Corneille (Commodore), Le Rhin, L'Uranie,* and *La Thamise,* were discovered about five miles astern; all sail was immediately crowded upon our little squadron, steering about S. S.W. with a moderate breeze from the W. N.W.; as the day broke, the *Redbridge* schooner hove in sight on the larboard bow upon the opposite tack, having a transport under her convoy, and, passing within hail of the *Phoebe*, soon after spoke me.

The lieutenant recommended my tacking and following him; but as I saw that by so doing I should be running into the teeth of the enemy, and inevitably taken in a quarter of an hour, I preferred executing my captain's orders by keeping my station as long as I could: to this end we cut the long boat adrift, and began to lighten the vessel by throwing the cargo overboard, and setting every yard of canvas that could stand ; but, notwithstanding all our efforts, the enemy a was rapidly gaining both on myself and on the *Phoebe*, and escape for either appeared impossible.

Seeing the *Redbridge* persevere in endeavouring to cross them, it occurred to me that Captain Capel might probably have directed the lieutenant to take the prizes under his convoy, and stand to the northward, in order to create a diversion, and thereby separate the pursuing enemy; this idea was strengthened by observing the weathermost open her fire upon the schooner soon after, which immediately struck, and, together with the other *settée*, hove to.

The time lost in exchanging prisoners, indicating no very

zealous anxiety to resume the chase, also tended to confirm the impression; hence, doubting whether I had not erred in neglecting the advice (for it did not amount to an order) of the lieutenant of the *Redbridge*, I determined on bearing up, in the hope of getting to leeward, and enticing one of the frigates after me.

At this time I was about three miles on the weather bow, and the *Phoebe* about four ahead of the French squadron. Scarcely were the sails trimmed, and the impossibility of escape obvious, than I determined on running the vessel athwart hawse of the head-most, in the hope of doing some mischief, and thereby facilitating the escape of the *Phoebe*; but this design was frustrated by our own helmsman, who, being a Frenchman,[1] and alarmed at the enemy's threat to sink us, disobeyed my orders in the conning[2] of the vessel.

Seeing her spring to, I ran aft and seized the helm, but it was too late, our rigging just cleared the main chains of the frigate, which, to my utter astonishment, hove to, and sent a boat to take possession; thus, by a voluntary and unnecessary act, did the enemy execute that, which I had fondly hoped to effect, and which was almost the only thing that could afford consolation in so painful a situation; for, notwithstanding I was myself a prisoner, I could not but indulge in feelings of triumph at seeing the *Phoebe* walk off in the face of a superior and much faster sailing foe.

As the other frigates closed, they also hove to, thus allowing the *Phoebe* to make one of the most miraculous escapes that occurred during the war. In the mean time the *Corneille* captured the transport. About half an hour was occupied in removing the prisoners and despatching the prizes to Toulon: during which period, the *Phoebe* was manoeuvring in defiance, firing guns and making signals as if communicating with a friendly force.

The chase was renewed, and an officer ordered to the mast head to look out, who reported that he saw several large sail to

---

1. This man went by the name of John Powell, he belonged to the *Phoebe's* Sailmaker's Crew, was sent on board the prize to repair the sails, and was to have been returned to the ship. I afterwards gave him a certificate of baptism for Plymouth, and passing himself as of Guernsey parents, he was never found out.
2. Directing the steering.

windward; the signal "a fleet in sight," was immediately made to the commodore, and soon after the squadron bore up for Toulon; on approaching which, Admiral Gantheaume, the commander-in-chief, by signal, ordered the chase to be resumed, evidently disapproving of the return; but the *Phoebe* was then some distance to windward. Captain Capel, seeing the irresolution and want of energy in the French squadron, about four p. m. boldly bore down, fired at them, and hauled his wind again, as if desirous of enticing them off shore; between six and seven p. m. they gave up the chase, and again made sail for Toulon, followed by the *Phoebe*.

It is impossible to say with what discretionary power the commodore was invested, but it was nevertheless certain, from the decided advantage the French squadron had in sailing, that if they had continued the chase in either instance, the *Phoebe* must have been taken, for there was no friendly ship of war within many leagues.

During the night the squadron lay to off the mouth of the harbour, and when day dawned, again gave chase, which was continued all day, taking care not to reach too far off shore; in the evening they bore up and lay to as before. On the 6th they again stood to sea, and returning, about sunset, anchored in Toulon roads.

The pleasurable feelings of curiosity which every seaman experiences on entering a port which he has never before visited, were absorbed in the recollection that I was a prisoner, cut off from my country and friends, fit the breaking out of a war, when I had served nearly seven years, expecting soon to join the *Victory*, and had buoyed myself up with the hope that I was on the very eve of promotion; these reflections, together with the conviction that I was so guarded as to preclude a probability of escape, tended to cast a temporary gloom over my spirits, and render me indifferent to the beauties of the surrounding scenery.

The following day we were separately examined before officers sent on board for the purpose, and our refusal to answer questions put to us, respecting the strength and situation of Lord Nelson, was construed into contempt, and so excited the rage of the captain of the *Rhin*, that he told us we were pirates; this novel information did not in the least disconcert us, for we suspected the ignorance of the man, and afterwards learnt he had been a barber; indeed, the whole tenor of his conduct evinced the dreadful convulsion which society in France must have undergone during the revolution, for such an ignorant, low-bred fellow to have risen to the command of a frigate.

When, however, it was explained to him that midshipmen in the British navy never had commissions, he resumed his composure, and, on my producing Captain Capel's written order, I was dismissed. Whitehurst and Murray underwent similar examinations, but with no better success.

During the twenty-one days we were on board the *Rhin* (under quarantine) the *Phoebe* frequently hove in sight, and, as we were informed, made repeated proposals for an exchange of prisoners, but unfortunately, the enemy were too well satisfied with such living proofs of their prowess in naval arms, to accede to them.

We were occasionally permitted to take exercise in the quarantine ground, until the morning of the 26th of August, when Murray, Whitehurst, and myself, together with the master of the *Transport* and ninety men, were landed about two miles to the westward of the town; thus separating us from the officers of the schooner, who consisted of Lieutenant M'Kenzie of the *Maidstone*, passenger, and six midshipmen; Lieutenant Lempriere, the commander of the schooner, having been drowned in the roads, by the upsetting of a boat.

Our separation from these officers, we supposed to have been caused by our contumacious refusal to give information about Lord Nelson, to the august barber; for we were told that we did not deserve to be treated like our comrades, and therefore were sent with the men.

On landing, we were received by a captain's guard of infantry, who very uncourteously pushed us indiscriminately into ranks, and, forming themselves in file on each side, with a few in front and rear, waited only the order to march, which was soon announced by a brace of dismal drums at the head of the escort, previous notice being given, through the medium of the interpreter, that the first who dared to wander from the ranks, would be shot.

It was really ludicrous to witness the parade of triumph evinced by our commanding officer, and the readiness with which his every gesture was imitated by some of his obsequious subordinates, who liberally dealt out blows with the flat of their swords upon the shoulders of anyone who from awkwardness or otherwise might step out of the direct line of march.

In this way we trudged along, each with a loaf of ammunition bread slung over the shoulder, no change of apparel, and only four dollars (which Whitehurst happened to possess) amongst us; occasionally we halted to rest, until about four p. m. when we were drummed in form through a village, and then countermarched, for the purpose of being drawn up in front of a large swinery, from which we witnessed the expulsion of pigs, sheep, and goats, to make room for us.

In the course of an hour, the lieutenant gave us (the three midshipmen) leave to dine in the village, attended by a sergeant, but even this incurred the displeasure of his brutal captain. We soon afterwards returned to the place of confinement, and remained nearly smothered in dust and dirt, until the morning, when we were again mustered into ranks, and after receiving a black loaf and seven-pence halfpenny each, as five days' pay, were drummed, as before, out of the village.

Our march was through a rugged country the scenery of which was very picturesque. The captain of the escort, generally keeping the interpreter by his side, occasionally (through him) entered into conversation with one or other of us; availing ourselves of a favourable opportunity, when apparently he was a little less morose than usual, we endeavoured to obtain permission to walk by ourselves, instead of being restricted to the ranks; but he was deaf to our request.

The Animals turned out to make way for the Prisoners

We ceased to wonder that he should evince so little feeling for our situation, when he related story after story of the bloody deeds committed during the reign of terror, in which it seemed, by his own account, he had been a frequent and willing actor. He and the captain of the *Rhin* were, probably, fair specimens of the set of hardened miscreants which the revolution had produced, and served to shew, that in those troublesome times, abandonment of principle and display of turpitude, no less than of talent, led the way to promotion and rank,

The third night we arrived at Aix, and were confined in what appeared to have been an old convent, in the yard of which, being permitted to range, we seized the opportunity of washing our linen, and were much pleased to learn, that we were no longer to be escorted by that inhuman offspring of tumult, who had had charge of us from Toulon. He resigned us to the care of a venerable old officer, whose first act of kindness was to inquire in what manner we had been treated by his predecessor, and who seemed indignantly surprised that no distinction had been made between the officers and the men.

The knowledge of this unmerited and unjust severity excited his warmest sympathy, and called forth the exercise of those nobler feelings, which could only flow from a natural benevolence of heart, for whilst his kindness and attentions were unbounded, his affability and cheerfulness made us almost forget that we were prisoners. "*Voyons, soyez gais,*" observed this good old gentleman, "the day may come when you may think yourselves happy in having been prisoners."

Although I gave him full credit for his philosophy, and the benevolence which prompted the observation, and felt grateful for our change of treatment, yet the result proved him to be no prophet; for I have never had cause to rejoice at an event which kept me so many years back in the service; however, so it was, and I. took advantage of my situation by endeavouring to learn something of the language, in occasional conversation with the interpreter; the next day's march brought us to a dirty village, where the church was our prison for the night.

On the 1st of September, we reached Tarascon, and were locked up in the tower; before the old officer took leave, he ordered the jailor to place us in a comfortable room by ourselves, and treat us as officers, though not on parole, that being contrary to the order from Toulon. In the morning he took us for a walk through the town, and in the afternoon sent a boy with us up the river, where we enjoyed a refreshing bath; after washing and drying our linen, we reluctantly returned to prison.

This was the first time since our capture that we had been without a guard, and might have easily decamped, had we been so inclined; but certainly no opportunity, however tempting, could have induced us to violate the frank and friendly confidence reposed in us by our philosophical veteran; in the evening he again visited us, and with much feeling, recommended us to the particular indulgence of his successor, who, for the sake of distinction, was dubbed "the fat captain". Early the following day, we passed through Beaucaire, and, arriving in the evening at Nismes, were marched to prison; some English gentlemen, here residing as *détenus*, kindly interfered in our behalf, and we were permitted to stroll about the streets till dark;

The next morning we breakfasted with a Mr. Walker, at whose house we had the good fortune to meet Doctor Grey,[3] from whom we received the kindest attention; we dined with him on that day, and those who have the happiness of his acquaintance, will best judge of the pleasure we experienced on that occasion; certainly his ravenous guests did ample justice to his genuine hospitality.

During our sojourn at Nismes, the nationality of Englishmen was conspicuously shewn forth in the assiduous attention of the *détenus* towards their captive countrymen; indeed, they considerably allayed the ennui and mortification of captivity, by confidently assuring us, that an exchange of prisoners had been arranged between the two governments, and that in six weeks we might rest satisfied of a happy return to the service of our country. In the full expectation of this desirable event, I

---

3. Now Sir Thomas Grey, residing at Ramsgate.

availed myself of every opportunity, in the mean time, of acquiring some trifling knowledge of the French language. They also made a subscription for the men, which I distributed amongst them in equal proportions.

About this time, Mr. Danderson, the master of the Transport, was kind enough to cash Whitehurst a draft for twenty pounds, by which means we fared much better. Proceeding on our journey, in two days we reached Montpellier, and were delivered into the hands of the commandant, for the night, who ordered us to be confined in the citadel. This was in so ruinous a state, that we might have decamped with little difficulty; the subject was mentioned to me, but my hope of an early exchange (in which the right of being included was then understood to be forfeited by an attempt to escape), our total ignorance of the country, of the means of embarking, and of the language, induced me to think it unadvisable. Could I have foreseen what followed, I should have decided differently; nevertheless, my services were offered, but no attempt was made.

From Montpellier we proceeded to Beziers, then to Narbonne; through Carcassone, Castelnaudary, Ville Franche, and several villages, until we arrived at Toulouse, on the 12th of September, when we were again placed at the head of the ranks, and drummed in triumph to the town hall. After remaining about an hour, surrounded by military and an immense populace, the guard was withdrawn, and we were desired to consider ourselves on parole; permission was given to take lodgings in the town, and we were further directed to apply for a passport, whenever we felt disposed to go beyond the suburbs.

The general, on being asked if our paroles were to be signed, replied, "No; a British officer values his honour too much, to render his signature necessary." When this was communicated to us, it may easily be imagined with what patriotic importance the compliment to our national character was received; with what feelings of pride his Britannic Majesty's midshipmen resolved to merit the eulogium of the enemy. On being told we might retire, the crowd fell back, opening a lane with a degree of civility and politeness that somewhat surprised us: we then strolled up the nearest street, for all were alike to us, not knowing where to go, or what to do. To those who have never quitted their own fire-sides, our situation at this moment may seem to have been desolate enough:—without friends; without experience; without any knowledge of the language of those, amongst whom the fate of war had thrown us.

But sailors are not prone to despondency; and the buoyancy of youthful spirits kept us from dwelling upon present difficulties, or anticipating future troubles. There was, at any rate, a novelty in our circumstances not wholly devoid of pleasure, and to which we were, in some measure, reconciled, by the knowledge that we were no longer subject to the caprice and insult of a military upstart, but enjoying, at least, a partial ray of liberty.

Scarcely had we reached a cross street, when, as gazing around in the perplexity of indecision which way to turn, a gentleman came up, and, addressing us in English, volunteered his services in seeking a lodging; after rambling about some time, as if begging an entrance at every door, we succeeded in hiring a room at nine *livres* per month, in one of the bye lanes; the furniture of which consisted of a bed, not untenanted, three chairs, and a table. In this hovel Whitehurst, Murray, and myself existed three weeks; at the expiration of that period, our pay being augmented to twenty-five sols per day, we were enabled to dine at a *table-d' hôte,* and get into a more comfortable lodging, with the additional luxury of a bed each.

Mr. Fitzsimons (the gentleman who procured us our first lodging) introduced me to a family of the name of Prevost, with whom he resided. It was from Mr. Fitzsimons that I learnt the first rudiments of the French language; but I was still more indebted to Mrs. Prevost, an accomplished and pleasing lady, who took infinite pains to instruct me, and by whose flattering influence I was encouraged to apply so closely to my studies, that in two months I was able to make myself understood.

My comrades were also studying French, and making rapid improvement; so that, each stimulating the other to exertion in our new pursuit, we seldom thought of amusements till the evening. Being considered as military officers, we were allowed the privilege of going to the theatre upon paying four shillings and eight-pence per month; this was not only an agreeable, but a profitable lounge, and we seldom neglected to attend. On the arrival of Messrs. M'Kenzie, Blakeney, Temple, Maxwell, Barklay, and Edwards, the officers taken in the *Redbridge*, several of them joined our *table-d'hôte*, and we mustered rather a large and merry party.

With respect to society, I was more fortunate than my companions, as I frequently dined, and passed my evenings, at the Prevosts'. In the beginning of October, I received a remittance from my father, by which our means were so materially increased, that we no longer confined ourselves to short commons, but indulged in comforts to which we had long been strangers.

During our stay in this once noble capital, we passed some cheerful days, and being in continual expectation of an exchange of prisoners, were the more anxious to acquire the language, before orders arrived to march us to the coast. The seamen were not so patient, for several of them attempted to escape; one party of fire, after marching and counter-marching fourteen days, supposed they had reached the neighbourhood of the Pyrenees; when, to their utter surprise and consternation, they found themselves within a few miles of the town; thus situated, and being half starved, they despaired of getting away, and delivered themselves up. Notwithstanding this failure, several others made similar attempts, but I recollect only one individual who did not return to prison; and his success was owing to his having preserved his American passport, which he had obtained when afloat, to protect him from the impress.

On the 2nd of December, orders having arrived for our removal, I waited on Mrs. Prevost, to take leave; after expressing sorrow at my departure, and hopes of return, she embraced me as tenderly as though I had been her own child. I left the house with gratitude and regret, and joined my comrades; after a few necessary arrangements, we bade a somewhat reluctant adieu to Toulouse. The marching party consisted of eleven, who, being now considered on parole, had no guard; but were accompanied by one *gendarme* to shew the road, and take the *feuille de route*; a cart was allowed to carry the baggage. We proceeded at discretion during three days, dined and slept at the different inns, like independent gentlemen, and enjoyed all the comforts our limited finances would afford.

On our arrival at Auch, about forty miles west of Toulouse, we hired lodgings, in different parties; six of us took up our quarters in the house of a *ci-devant* nobleman, who became particularly kind on all occasions. He frequently amused us with the relation of his adventures during the horrid times of blood and rapine; also with accounts of his subsequent travels; dwelling particularly on those in England, where he had passed some very happy days in high life.

He possessed all the distinguishing qualities of the gentleman, and all the communicative intelligence of the learned traveller, without any of that *gasconade*, that bombastic exaggeration, tending to self exaltation, for which the generality of French travellers are famed; indeed, his every act and expression, whether flowing from head or heart, evinced that nature had bestowed upon him her choicest gifts, in bountiful profusion. During our stay at Auch, we had unrestricted liberty, and could ramble about the country at pleasure.

On the 11th of December, an order arrived from Paris to send us to Verdun, in the department of La Meuse, and we were to set out the following day. Our finances being reduced to a very low ebb, we consulted our truly noble friend, who, not enduring the thought of our travelling such a distance, in the depth of winter, with nothing more than soldiers' allowance, persuaded the bankers to lend me twenty pounds on a draft; this timely supply gave new vigour to our spirits, and enabled us to fortify ourselves against the inclemencies of the weather.

At noon, we took leave of our worthy friend, and departed; and, arriving in the evening at Beaumont, we were very comfortably housed, yet strictly guarded.

The next day, reaching Montauban, after a tedious march, we were drawn up in line, in front of the town hall, and formally inspected by the commissary, who, with a studied politeness, enticed us into a prison by a most artful piece of duplicity, intended, no doubt, to wound our feelings; he was, however, disappointed in his hopes of annoyance, for we could not refrain from a general burst of laughter at the simple manner in which we had been entrapped.

On entering a room, which had been formed by the spade, we found the barred windows but a few feet above the surface of the water; it was only on one side that we had either light or air, and this attended by the refreshing vapours of the river, and the cooling dampness of the surrounding earth, oozing saltpetre from every pore.

We requested to be allowed to see the commandant, but to no effect; soon afterwards a lieutenant was sent to visit us, with whom we expostulated on our situation, observing, that in all civilized countries, officers, who had become prisoners of war were put upon parole, and that during our march in France, we had never, until now, experienced treatment which was worthy only of the days of Robespierre. He was somewhat nettled at the remark, and told us, he was desired by the commandant, to say, that he was himself once a prisoner in England, and that, from having been confined in Porchester castle, he had sworn to retaliate; that, exclusive of his oath, he had the most unlimited confidence in the British officers, but that he judged it prudent to have a little security also. This fellow, like his commissary, another of those *parvenus* sprung from the very dregs of the people, and actuated by pitiful motives of revenge, kept us immured in this most unhealthy hole, during the following day.

On the morning of the 15th, we departed, with a different guard, and in the evening were comfortably billeted in a village. The next day, proceedings on our journey, we arrived, at a late hour, at Cahors. Thence we marched northwardly. Nothing occurred worth notice, but the loss of the guards, who had fallen asleep in drunkenness; we, however, marched on without them.

On the 19th, we slept at Gourdon; on the 20th, at Martel; and on the 21st, after marching over rocks and hills, in a wretched country, broke suddenly upon a most beautiful view over an extensive and rich valley, in the centre of which rises the town of Brive. Scarcely had we sat down to dinner at this place, when we were surprised by the *gendarmes*, who, from a state of consternation on account of the apprehended loss of their prisoners, became as much elated when they found we were all present.

On the 22nd, notwithstanding the weather was stormy, we were obliged to proceed, but, by the consent of the guards, hired mules, and got that night into Uzerches, a distance of about thirty-five miles; the next day we reached Limoges, and were conducted to the door of the prison; but there making a firm stand, in spite of the threats of the colonel, succeeded in obtaining permission from the general to be quartered in an inn. A strong guard of veterans was, however, sent to surround the house.

Here we remained the 24th; on the 25th, when preparing to depart, a long bill was presented, with the expenses of the gendarmes included, and it was with much difficulty we could convince our host, that, not having invited them to guard us, we had too much urbanity to offer so gross an insult to the colonel, as to pay for his guests, and therefore desired that the demand might be made upon him; this so incensed these members of the legion of honour, that they swore it should cost us dear; however, nothing ill grew out of it.

Journeying on and halting occasionally as inclination urged, we ate our Christmas dinner in a miserable village, where we stopped for the night

In this manner we trudged on two days, and on the third, a dispute arose between the landlord and our commissariat department, in consequence of the nefarious impositions of the former, when the mayor interposed and cast us with costs. During the dispute, I entered an adjoining bedroom, and observing on the mantle various little images in plaster of Paris, in the midst of which was the bust of the adored Buonaparte, and no one being near, I could not resist the temptation of placing its head downwards, in a vessel which was no ornament to a mantle-piece, nor usually found there; the arrangement of the images I also altered, so as to make them appear ridiculing this misfortune of the *premier consul*. In the midst of my amusement, the order of march was given and I hurried out unseen.

We journeyed on about six leagues with a morose set of gendarmes, who, on entering a public house in the evening, made private arrangements with the host to impose on the prisoners. In consequence of an attempt to frustrate this iniquitous design, we were enticed from the tavern, entrapped by an artifice similar to the one practised at Montauban, and locked up in an unfurnished house, with nothing but straw and short commons.

We, nevertheless, joked away the hours in good humour, preferring present inconvenience to the more agreeable comforts of a tavern, attended by imposition and insolence. Proceeding on our journey, we were occasionally lodged in a tavern or a prison, at the caprice of the guard; who happily, on the 29th, were superseded by a more rational set. These we instantly began to flatter, and to abuse their predecessors; a generally successful method of turning to account the proverbial vanity of such people, and which here had the desired effect.

On our arrival at Argenton, I purchased of one of my companions an old horse for 12s 6d; this poor jaded animal afforded amusement for several days, till at length I sold him for 3s 6d.

We quitted this town on the 1st of January, 1804, and passing through a beautiful country reached Chateauroux, and there remained the following day. The *gendarmes*, whom flattery had so much influenced, now left us; and notwithstanding they recommended us to their successors as *de braves gens*, we experienced different treatment; they frequently spoke harshly and insolently, hinting at the same time that we had not conducted ourselves properly.

This being unintelligible, and having often found on such occasions a deportment bordering on *hauteur* to produce the best effects with the *canaille*, we scarcely noticed them. In the evening we entered a public house, and on passing through the kitchen, observed the entrance of an adjoining prison, and suspecting it was intended for our quarters, a feint of resistance was made; it was, however, a fruitless effort, and we were compelled to enter. In vain we remonstrated, and assured them they would be punished for disobeying the order of the general at Auch, relative to our treatment, which had been shewn to us by the late guard.

They became excessively enraged, and, at length, one said, "You are in prison by a counter-order lately received from Auch, for having put Buonaparte's head into a *pot-de-chambre.*"

A silent gaze of astonishment was followed by sudden gusts of laughter, which so thundered through the prison, as to drown the voice of the incensed orator; and nothing could be heard but "*Buonaparte,*" and "*Diable.*" The louder he spoke the more boisterous was our mirth, until, frantic with rage, he drew his sword, rushed forward and thrust it through the grated hole in the door, stamped, and swore in such a foaming passion, that when the storm of derision was over, he could scarcely articulate:—

"Each passion dimm'd his face,
"Thrice changed with pale ire, envy, and despair."

It was some time before we ceased laughing at this truly ridiculous event, for we had forgotten the boyish frolic alluded to, and had not the least idea that it could be thought of sufficient importance to cause an official report, and an order by a *courier de la republique,* that we should be cast into prison. No sooner had the *gendarmes* retired, than the jailor supplied us with clean straw, and set his family cooking, so that we fared very well, in this otherwise miserable den.

On the 4th, 5th, and 6th, we marched on, and, in default of prisons, were quartered in the public houses.

On the 7th, we arrived at Orleans, and were joined by Lieutenant Prater, of the second West India regiment, captured on his passage from Honduras to England. The next day we proceeded to Pethivier. Here our fare was wretched enough; short commons, and a truss of straw, in a small tower, were our accommodation for the night

On the 11th, we journeyed on to Melun, where again, in the other extreme, we were lodged in a comfortable inn, and permitted to stroll about the town without the least interruption, and even without a *gendarme*.

The 12th was a *jour de repos*. Whether it was thought too great an honour for us to pass so near *la bonne ville de Paris,* or not, I cannot say; but instead of taking the direct road to Verdun, the next day our course was shaped to the S. E. and we slept at Belleville; thence eastwardly, and dined in a village, where the *gendarmes* again attempted to make us pay for escort, but we had travelled too far to be such dupes.

On our arrival at Troyes, the following day, the guard was about to conduct us to prison, when we insisted upon halting at an inn, until the pleasure of the general should be known; finding they wavered at our firmness, we desired that one of the *gendarmes* should conduct two of us to his house, where we had an immediate interview. Instead of receiving us with the contemptible pomp of a mushroom general, he immediately presented chairs, and, with the mild dignity of the accomplished gentleman, expressed his approbation of our request to be considered on parole, gave the necessary directions to the *gendarme*, and ordered him to retire. He then said, if we were desirous to remain in the town a few days, the permission should be granted; but, as our finances and inclination were not in unison, we declined his kind offer, with many thanks.

We returned to our friends, elated with the success of our mission; all participated in the pleasure, not merely from having escaped the filth and vermin of a prison, but also from its giving us a certain degree of consequence in the eyes of the *gendarmes*, who afterwards became somewhat more respectful in their deportment It may not be irrelevant here to insert a remark which struck us forcibly at the time, that when we met with an officer of the *ancien règime*, we were generally treated with kindness, but when under those sprung up from the revolutionary *canaille*, known, in France, by the appellation of *enfans de terrour*, we, on the contrary, met with insolence and severity.

We left Troyes on the 16th, and halted to breakfast in a village, when the remains of my twenty pounds were expended on a scanty meal. Lieutenant M'Kenzie, seeing that the reduced circumstances of our party now compelled us to keep aloof from the dinner table, most handsomely insisted that his remaining cash should be shared amongst us, so that, by his liberality, we again fared very well. This was not the only instance of his kind, interference in my behalf.

He also had been harshly treated by the *gendarmes*; on one occasion, they threatened to lash him to a horse's tail, if he did not walk faster, which put his Scotch blood into such a state of fermentation, that it was with difficulty his friends could prevent a personal attack on the commanding officer; thus his utter detestation and abhorrence, at that time, of everything French was sealed; indeed he carried them to such a pitch, that he vowed he would not even study the language, lest it might tend to abate his determined hatred; but such feelings were not the natural productions of his benevolent heart; they had been planted there by insolence and oppression, which his noble mind could scarcely endure: all who know him will unite in declaring him worthy of the compliment of the poet—

"The patriot virtues that distend thy thought,
"Spread on thy front, and in thy bosom glow."

The 19th, we halted at Chalons, on the Marne; the 20th, at St. Menehould; and, on the 21st, in spite of very bad weather, reached the end of our journey—the long wished for Verdun.

We were escorted to the citadel; when certain regulations, as the conditions of my parole, were given to me for perusal. These I signed. Permission was then granted me to retire into the town, where I took lodgings suitable to my finances. I found about 400 English and a constant influx for several days.

I shall not fatigue the reader with a repetition of those occurrences in Verdun which have already appeared before the public, in various shapes, but confine myself to the leading features of the discipline of the depôt, and a few other particulars which may not be altogether uninteresting.

But I shall first recall to mind, that on the renewal of hostilities, in 1803, Buonaparte detained all British subjects, between the ages of nine and sixty, throughout the republican dominions, as an alleged act of retaliation for the seizure of French merchant vessels, on the immediate declaration of war. Whether the blow preceded or followed the word, might be said to be nothing to a midshipman; the result proved, that it concerned him very materially, inasmuch as there was in consequence no exchange of prisoners. But, as it is equally unnecessary, and contrary to my inclination to give an opinion upon that political subject, I shall keep within the limits I have marked out for myself, and state, that the unfortunate Englishmen who had been thus captured, were denominated *déténus*, without the benefit of any stipend for their maintenance.

In the autumn of 1803, the several depôts of these *déténus*, and of officers on parole, were concentrated in Verdun; the command of which was entrusted to a man named Wirion, who had been an adroit police officer, but, during the revolution, under the auspices of Bernadotte, rose rapidly to the rank of general of *gendarmerie*. No sooner had this man entered upon his new office, than he established a system of "espionage," in imitation of the police of the whole republic

It was computed that he had no less than fifty principal informers, on whom he could depend, and each of these had one or more subordinate reporters, besides the eighty gendarmes, who (one *marshal de logis* [4] excepted) may be added to that number; many of them also employed the tradesmen, women, and servants, to collect their gleanings. Wirion thereby frequently acquired the earliest intimation of things, which we fancied unknown to many of our friends.

Had Buonaparte carefully searched his army list, he could not have found two men less calculated to preside over a body

---

4. Old Tisserand.

of gentlemen, than the General Wirion and the Commandant Courçelles;[5] the only distinction between them being, that to the depravity, of an unprincipled rapacious tyrant, the latter added the malice and manners of a ruffian. The prolific genius of both was continually on the rack to invent new means of accumulating wealth, alike indifferent to justice or honour; variable and capricious, they would sometimes refuse to take cognizance of outrageous acts; whilst at others, insignificant trifles would be visited with severity: these vacillations depending principally upon the power of the aggressing individual to con tribute to their coffers.

Nevertheless, every candid mind will confess, that during Wirion's administration, the personal treatment of the prisoners (setting aside extortion) was generally apportioned to individual desert, and if occasional acts of oppression occurred, they were exceptions emanating rather from the petty malice of vulgar minds, unaccustomed to exercise authority, than the result of systematic discipline.

Prisoners on their arrival in Verdun were invariably conducted to the citadel, when their names, age, birth-place, profession, and description, were entered in a book. They were then obliged to sign a paper, promising upon honour to conform to the regulations of the depot, and not to escape, if permitted to reside in the town. A direct violation of this engagement was so unreservedly condemned by all classes, that during the five first years of the war, I recollect but three who so disgraced their country; for those determined to depart generally committed an offence, which would insure deprivation of parole—it being generally considered that the instant any one was taken into custody by armed men, no matter from what cause, parole ceased.

Nor can this practice, where it produced actual imprisonment, be condemned, when it is considered, that the prisoners were devoid of even a hope of exchange. Nevertheless, it was not without its evils, for it became difficult to define the exact

---

5. Courçelles was Commandant of the Department of La Meuse, and of the fortress of Verdun, and resided in the citadel.

line of distinction between open violation and this alternative; to wit—an offence so trifling, but so exactly measured, was contrived as to induce a *gendarme* to take the parties into custody, and lodge them in the guard-room, until he had reported the occurrence to the lieutenant; in the mean time, they stepped out of the window, and concealed themselves in the town till dark, and then departed.

This might be fair enough with the *détenus*, because they were made prisoners in open Violation of all law, justice, or honour, but with prisoners of war it was justly ridiculed and condemned; to say the least of it, it was a bad augury: for the germ of honour buds in the spring of our days, and if at that epoch an officer wounds her opening flowers, she seldom ripens to maturity: or, in other words, the neglect of the minutest part of this delicate and noble feeling in early life, generally leads to a more flagrant breach in the later hour of temptation.

Various permissions, such as ranging six miles from the town, living in the country, and a few others, were after-indulgences, not contained in the conditions of parole, but frequently obtained by the intervention of a *douceur*. The principal regulations were as follow: signing in a book at the *appel*, according to rank, *viz*. captains in the navy, and field officers, once a month; lieutenants, every five days; midshipmen, and others, twice a day; (thus calculating the word of a midshipman as equal only to one sixtieth part of that of a field officer;) the neglect of this regulation was atoned for by the payment of two shillings and sixpence each time. The returning into town was enjoined whenever a gun was fired, this being the signal of desertion, and also every evening at sunset, previous to the shutting of the gates.

Our place of abode was registered in the books, and we were, therefore, obliged to give notice whenever we thought proper to remove.

The commissioned officers had the privilege of drawing quarterly bills for their pay. Buonaparte gave express orders that English bills should not be negotiated; this was acted upon for a time, during which the officers lived on French allowance: but afterwards, they got their bills cashed, at a discount of twenty-five per cent. Midshipmen received, every month, from the senior officer, half of their pay, but subject to a diminution of from ten to twenty-five percent. Besides the above, a monthly allowance was received from the French government, as follows:—

	£. s. d.
Colonels and post captains	4. 0. 0.
Majors and commanders	3. 0. 0.
Captains in the army, and lieutenants in the navy	2. 0. 0.
Lieutenants in the army, clergymen, and pursers	1.10. 0.
Midshipmen, ensigns, warrant officers, and masters of merchant vessels	1. 5. 0.

The *détenus*, holding military rank, received the same pay as prisoners of war, but the civilians nothing. The needy civilians, however, received from the managers of the patriotic fund, something every month, proportionate to their families; so that after the first year or two, there were but very few who suffered, except from their own misconduct.

There were well-regulated public schools established at the expense of the above fund, at all the principal depots; and at Verdun there were two, one of which was for young gentlemen. These schools proved of infinite benefit; since by means of them not only were the boys trained up to industrious habits, but many of the steady seamen learned to read and write, and also acquired a considerable knowledge of the principles of navigation. These, in turn, not unfrequently became tutors to others; such pursuits afforded an amusing occupation to many, and considerably diminished the irksomeness of hours, which must otherwise have been intolerably tedious and hateful.

From the incongruous mixture of all ranks and fortunes in Verdun, there arose a diversity of humour and eccentricity, from which frequent quarrelling and duelling might have been expected; but considering that there were assembled, under the most distressing circumstances, about one thousand persons of all pursuits, devoid of even a hope of restoration to liberty, duels but seldom occurred: not more than three or four proved fatal during the eleven years of the war; and those which took place, appeared to proceed more from fashionable compulsion than from any revengeful desire of reparation; the cause of almost every quarrel could be traced to gambling, wine, or women.

There was, however, one duel worth mentioning; two mids, both under fourteen years of age, were found shooting at each other across a table in their lodging, and nothing but the bursting open the door, and forcibly taking their pistols from them put an end to the combat

Amongst the various allurements to iniquity, the gambling-table, otherwise termed "hell," was the most notorious, because sanctioned as legal, and regularly attended by a body of *gendarmes* to maintain order; for which General Wirion, notwithstanding he was one of the proprietors of the funds, which amounted to 200*l*, levied a fine of 100*l* per month. The principal games were *rouge et noir*, and *roulette*. The Satan of this gang of robbers made himself acquainted with the affairs of almost everyone in the depôt, and well knew to whom he could lend money with safety; he was constantly on the watch to ensnare the unwary and inebriated, which practice had taught him to do, under the specious mask of friendship, without creating suspicion.

I cannot refrain from reciting an awful instance of the consequences of a man becoming his own master too early in life, and placing too much confidence in his own powers to withstand the snares of temptation in the society of the profligate. An unfortunate young surgeon's assistant, in order to while away the tedious hours, after a party, was enticed into this sink of iniquity, and tempted to throw on the table a half-crown; he won, and repeated the experiment several evenings successfully, till at length he lost.

The manager immediately offered him a *rouleau* of fifty pounds, which, in the warmth of play, he thoughtlessly accepted and lost. He then drew a bill on his agent, which Captain Brenton [6] endorsed, this he also lost; he drew two others, which met

---

6. Now Sir Jahleel Brenton.

the same fate; and the next morning he was found dead in his bed, with his limbs much distorted and his fingers buried in his sides. On his table was found an empty laudanum bottle, labelled "L———'s cure for all diseases," and scraps of paper whereon he had been practising the signature of Captain Brenton. On inquiry, it was found that he had forged that officer's name to the two last bills. Thus did a once respectable young man meet a most dreadful and disgraceful end, from, being exposed, at too early a period in life, to the temptation of gambling.

Another circumstance also occurred, the atrocity of which was somewhat tinged with the ludicrous. A clerk named Chambers losing his monthly pay, which was his all, at the gambling-table, begged to borrow of the managers; but they knew his history too well to lend without security, and therefore demanded something in pawn;—

"I have nothing to give," replied the youth, "but my ears."—

"Well," said one of the witty demons, "let us have them;" the youth immediately took out of his pocket a knife, and actually cut off all the fleshy part of one of his ears, and threw it on the table to the astonishment of the admiring gamesters; he received his two dollars and gambled on. When this circumstance was reported to the senior officer, the hero was sent to Bitche.[7]

These were not the only instances of the pernicious effects of public gambling: some were led on from one vice to another until totally ruined; while others, in despair and to drown their sorrows, destroyed themselves by drinking and other debaucheries. The town was not purified of its grand sources of corruption, until Buonaparte, in 1806, abolished the tables. As a proof that these swindling managers visited Verdun solely to defraud the English, the following notice was placed upon the door of the gaming-house:—

> "This bank is established for the accommodation of the English; all Frenchmen are forbidden to play."

---

7. Bitche, termed by the prisoners the "Castle of Tears" was a depôt of punishment; a strong fortress not far from the Rhine, in the department of the Lower Rhine, built on an immense rock, having numerous subterraneous caves, bomb-proof.

When such was the unblushing avowal, one cannot be surprised at the number of atrocities, peculations, and extortions of those: in authority. I have taken some trouble in making the subjoined calculations, for the perfect accuracy of which it would be impossible to vouch, from the difficulty of ascertaining the facts; but, judging from what was made public, I shall be very near the truth when I lay the plunder, extorted by the military authority from the English, at about 30,000*l*; to say nothing of that by the civil power, nor of the extortions of Jews, money-dealers, and the trades-people in general; for the English appeared fair game for all, and he that could rob them most was the most envied. But not having so wide a field wherein to exercise this peculiar talent, no one could cope with the gallant general. The following circumstance may first be noticed, as a specimen of his delicacy.

FINES EXTORTED FROM THE PRISONERS.

	£.	*s.*	*d.*
For missing the "appels," 2*s.* 6*d.* each, and permission to sign the books at your lodgings, yielding about 50*l.* per month, for three years	1800	0	0
Doctor's certificate to avoid regulations, 10*l.* per month, for five years	600	0	0
Sale of passports to go out of town; about 2000 issued in seven years, losses, &c.	250	0	0
For going out of town on horseback, or in carriage, 100 at 5*s.*	25	0	0
Permission to reside in the country, say average six for six years, at 10*s.* per month	216	0	0
Tax on four clubs, 1*l.* 5*s.* per month each, for six years	360	0	0
Carried forward	3251	0	0

	£	s.	d.
Brought forward	3251	0	0
Races, exclusive of extortions which grew out of them	180	0	0
Permission for servants to return to Verdun, at 12*l.* each, four a-year for six years	288	0	0
Permission for " détenus" to return to Verdun from Valenciennes	400	0	0
Gambling-houses, 100*l.* per month, for three years	3600	0	0
Difference between the franc and livre tournois in Wirion's time 720*l.*; in Courçelles's 240*l.*	960	0	0
Permission for masters of vessels and others to return to Verdun, during seven years	420	0	0
Stoppages of pay, for pretended dilapidations in the prisons	520	0	0
Defraying expenses of re-capture when attempting escape	300	0	0
Masters of merchantmen, permitted to reside in town, at 4*s.* each per month, part only collected .... £80 Ditto, on another occasion, 500 at 7*s.* 6*d.* each 187			
	267	0	0
Commandant Courçelles's wine, and other robberies, not mentioned	1000	0	0
Carried forward	11186	0	0

	£	s.	d.
Brought forward	11186	0	0
Courçelles's son, the jailor's, robberies	150	0	0
Corporal Latreille's confession of 100*l.*, for ten years	1000	0	0
Maréchal de Logis Bouillé, 150*l.* per annum, for five years	750	0	0
Lieutenant Massin, 100*l.* per annum, for two years	200	0	0
Licenses for various privileges	300	0	0
Lieutenant Demanget, 150*l.* for four years	600	0	0
One third of 1800 prisoners at Valenciennes were permitted to work in town, on paying 10 sols a-day for one year, producing 3912*l.* 10*s.*; then 5 sols for one year 1956*l.* 5*s.* ..	5868	15	0
	£20054	15	0
Calculating similar extortions at the ten other depôts each only at one-twentieth of that sum, amounts to	10027	7	6
	£30,082	2	6

After Sir Jahleel Brenton had been visiting the depôts, General Wirion told him, that, as an additional duty had devolved upon the *gendarmes*, in consequence of one of their companions being on duty with him, he (the general) would be glad if Sir Jahleel would make them a present.

He requested time to consider it, and soon afterwards returned armed with a golden *douceur*; he then told the general, that as he had travelled officially, at the expense of his own government, he must request a receipt as a voucher for this portion of his account. The general eyed him with a satanic grin, and replied, that in consideration of the kindness he had shewn to his attendant *gendarme*, he would not allow him to give anything.

Nor need the reader be sceptical upon this enormous amount: a highly esteemed friend has submitted my calculation of the separate items to a very distinguished officer, whose situation rendered him fully competent to judge; he considers that it is under the mark; though such calculations, from their very nature, cannot be very accurate.

I could adduce a multitude of facts in corroboration of their probable accuracy, but when the fate of those in authority over the prisoners is known, I trust all doubt on the subject will vanish.

As I do not intend to sully these pages with a recital of the separate atrocities of the Verdun worthies: I shall briefly insert a list of those who committed suicide, or were exposed by martial justice; in the hope their fate may prove a warning to future commandants, and a safeguard to the unfortunate.

Wirion—A general, and inspector-general of the Imperial *gendarmerie*, officer of the legion of honour, and commander-in-chief of the prisoners of war; shot himself.

Courçelles—Colonel and commandant of Verdun, and of the department of the Meuse, officer of the legion of honour; dismissed from the army.

Demanget—Lieutenant of *gendarmerie*, member of the legion of honour; dismissed from the army.

Massin—Lieutenant of *gendarmerie*, member of the legion of honour; shot himself.

Bouillé—Marèchal de logis of *gendarmerie*, paymaster, and member of the legion of honour; reduced to the ranks.

Name Forgotten—Lieutenant of *gendarmerie* at Sarre Louis; shot himself.

Name Unknown—A colonel at Montmedy, member of the legion of honour; condemned to the *gallies*.

Mundevellars—Captain in the army, *aide-de-camp* to General Wirion, member of the legion of honour; dismissed the army.

A Chef d' Escadron—Commandant at Bitche, member of the legion of honour, was denounced, but saved himself by obtaining from several of the prisoners a certificate of good conduct.

A Colonel at Valenciennes, dismissed.

Name Forgotten—*Aide-de-camp* to General Wirion, member of the legion of honour; dismissed the army.

Besides these honourable members so disgraced, many others narrowly escaped, and a long list of insignificant delinquents, might be added, whose rogueries are not comprised in the foregoing calculations.

In contradistinction to these notorious characters, most of whom sprung from the revolution, the names of De Beauchene and De Meulan need only be mentioned, to restore the equanimity of our temper; but in order to avoid breaking the thread of the Narrative, these high-minded and gallant soldiers will be reserved for the appendix.

The following circumstance, however, must not be omitted, because it has been incorrectly mentioned in other publications.

Four of us were rambling about the country, with a pointer and silken-net, when the signal-gun was fired; on our return, in passing through the village of Tierville, about two miles from Verdun, we were surprised by two *gendarmes*, one of whom, instantly dismounted, and seized me, uttering the most blasphemous epithets; he tied my elbows behind me, then slipping a noose round my neck, triced me up to the holsters of his saddle, remounted and returned with his prize to town, exulting in his cowardly triumph, and pouring forth volleys of vulgar abuse, every now and then tightening the cord, so as to keep me trotting upon the extremity of the toes to obtain relief, then again loosening it, as occasional guttural symptoms of strangulation seemed to indicate necessity.

Vain would be the attempt to convey an adequate idea of the

impotent rage then boiling within me, at the insult offered to my juvenile dignity, whilst a determined haughtiness disdained to betray the slightest indication of submission or complaint.

My companions were secured round the middle with the utmost violence and brutality. Thus we were conducted to town; and, when delivered over to the proper authorities and interrogated, were released. The next morning I waited on the senior officer. Captain Woodruff, who, with a promptitude which did honour to his feelings, and indignation worthy of a British officer, immediately represented the fact to General Wirion, who assured him the *gendarmes* should be ordered into solitary confinement.

In July, 1807, my intimate friend and brother-mid., Thomas Walbeoff Cecil, communicated to me his determination to attempt escape, and proposed my joining him: but as at that time it was quite impossible, he had recourse to another brother officer, named Gordon, who immediately consented, and dreparations were forthwith made. Our mutual and worthy friend, Ellison, furnished Cecil with the necessary funds.

Two of us walked out every day, and in the centre of a large wood, about five miles north of Verdun, concealed provisions, maps, and clothing. Cecil and Gordon, in order to divest themselves of parole, went to the theatre, and behaved ill, when they were arrested and confined in the guard-house; but disdaining to take advantage of a place not considered a prison, they waited till they were locked up in the *cachot* of the citadel; the night passed without being able to effect their object.

The next morning, they were unexpectedly marched off, with three others, under a strong escort, for Bitche. Ellison and I, on the lookout, joined the party ere they had passed the suburbs, and walked with them about six miles; when arrangements were made for their return to the rendezvous in the wood, should they be enabled to overpower or evade the guard, within a certain distance of Verdun. We returned to town; the offenders proceeded to their destination of punishment.

The next evening an express arrived of their escape. On the

opening of the gates, in the morning of the third day, Ellison and I hastened out to the rendezvous, and to our inexpressible joy there found our friends, accompanied by a youngster named Maxwell, exhausted with fatigue. Cecil related, that about an hour after we left them, the guard was relieved at the house of correspondence, between Verdun and Metz, but owing to some mistake, there arrived only one gendarme to take charge of five prisoners, whom, the better to secure, he placed in the cart with the luggage; until the ascending a steep hill, afforded Cecil, Gordon, and Maxwell the pretext to alight, to relieve the horse; their intentions being previously communicated to the other two, that all might decamp together: two declined; the other three, watching the opportunity, bolted across a ploughed field, for a wood, distant about five hundred yards; the gendarme immediately discharged his pistols at them, but durst not pursue. They gained the wood in safety, with the loss of one of Maxwell's shoes.

On the arrival of the cart in the first village, the whole male population were armed, and despatched to scour the woods; frequently, during the day, did some of these fellows pass within a few yards of them, but the thick foliage afforded protection. In this state of panting anxiety, they continued till dark, when they, debouched, and directed their steps to the appointed rendezvous; but purposely avoiding the roads, they missed their way, and their progress during the night was slow.

At dawn of day, there being no wood near, they concealed themselves in a corn-field; the sun pouring his burning rays full upon them, with scarcely a breath of wind, and no water, they suffered severely. In the afternoon they were surprised by a peasant, who I roughly ordered them out of his corn, when, faltering an excuse, they mildly tendered a remuneration for the damage they had done; this so moved him with compassion, that he I immediately offered to supply them with provisions and wine, and told them he knew they were the Englishmen everybody was seeking; but "fear not me," said he, "I will protect you;" and he departed.

In the mean time, Cecil watched his motions, and in about an hour observed him returning with the promised relief; they continued together till near dark. Just as they were about to separate, this good Samaritan, casting his eyes once more upon the thankful group, perceived that Maxwell had lost a shoe, he instantly took off one of his own, adding, "Here, my child, you shall not want a shoe whilst I have two;" nor could he be prevailed to to accept more than a trifle for his services. The usual reward for the recapture of Englishmen had no influence with honest poverty. Thus it may be said, that he fed the hungry, and clothed the naked, and never thought of recompense, but found it in the goodly act he performed. Soon afterwards, heartily wishing them success, he left them.

On quitting the corn, they travelled westerly, and reached the suburbs of Verdun at two a.m., forded the river, and gained the appointed rendezvous at four.

Ellison and I lost no time in returning to Verdun; procured more provisions, shoes, clothing, and 27 *louis*, and invited five of our friends to go out and partake of a *champetre* dinner with our fugitive brother officers.

We rejoined them about two p.m., and sat down to dinner on the grass, a jovial and merry party; what added to our glee, was the passing of General Wirion not far from us. About seven we parted company, and returned to my lodgings, where, to crown the propitious events of the day with boisterous mirth, we all enthusiastically drank "success to the lads of the forest," in a bumper of burgundy, out of the peasant's dirty old shoe: when it was unanimously resolved that it should be filled with silver, and returned to the owner, could he ever be traced out: but in this, notwithstanding repeated efforts, we never could succeed. From the sensation this tale excited, which, for months afterwards, was kept up by the production of the shoe at parties, in testimony of a generous soul, I have no hesitation in saying, that had he been found out, we should have had little difficulty in filling it even with gold.

The fugitives shaped their course to the eastward.

Unfortunately the dispositions of Cecil and Gordon did not then accord; they knew not each other, and the youth and inexperience of Maxwell, with, perhaps, the feeling that he was indebted to them both, prevented his interference, so that on the third day after leaving us, a dispute arose which led to a separation, by Cecil taking a road different from the one which most pleased Gordon. Scarcely had they parted one minute, when Cecil recollected he had an odd *louis* of the public fund in his possession; he immediately returned and offered it Gordon, who with equal spirit refused it. Maxwell, fearful of appearing to side with either, also refused it; so that this *louis* was placed upon a large stone in the middle of the road and there left.

Cecil resumed his favourite route, and proceeded through Germany to Trieste in the Gulf of Venice, and got home by the Mediterranean. Gordon and Maxwell marched through Prussia, and reached England by the North Seas. Both arrived in November, and, strange to tell, accidentally met in a coffee-house in London. Cecil, in singleness of heart, instantly advanced and offered Gordon his hand, which he refused; this renewed the quarrel, and they were bound over to keep the peace.

A few days subsequently Gordon was promoted, and as soon as he had joined his ship at Portsmouth he wrote to Cecil, repeating his challenge; there they met. Cecil received the shot of his adversary and then fired in the air, which so overcame Gordon, that gaining, as it were, a victory over himself, he instantly dashed his pistol to the earth, ran up, offered his hand, and apologized: at the same time accusing himself as the cause of all their disputes. Thus Gordon ceased to be blind to the worth of Cecil, and Cecil rejoiced to see a kindred feeling in the heart of Gordon; from that moment they became friends united in harmony and goodwill. This account I had from Gordon.

Gordon served about six years as lieutenant, and was promoted into the *Spider* brig, which soon afterwards was paid off. He then retired into private life, where, like most of his brother officers who had been guilty of surviving their interest, he was likely to remain, had he not volunteered to ship the turban and find out the source of the Nile. This quixotic scheme, undertaken alone, in despair of getting afloat, and in utter ignorance of the obstacles, or the means of surmounting them, was almost certain of failure. He was not, however, a man to be intimidated by the danger or difficulty of a task which most scientific men had deemed impossible; for the Nile, in all probability, has not one—but one hundred sources: on the contrary, they had charms which suited his romantic turn of mind, and the very idea of accomplishing what no one man had accomplished, was sufficient to goad him on to destruction; for it was morally certain he would perish—and he did perish.

Cecil was also promoted in December, 1807. In 1810 he was lieutenant of the *Tonant*, 80, under the *pro tempore* command of Captain Stackpole. Both were superseded in the early part of the following year; soon afterwards, Cecil met a midshipman named T——n, who had been with him in that ship. A friendly conversation ensued, when the mid. informed Cecil of Stackpole's appointment to the *Statira*, and asked if he would like to sail with him again—to which Cecil replied negatively, adding, "he draws too long a bow for me."

Soon after this circumstance, Captain Stackpole and the mid took a passage in the *Ganymede* to join the *Statira*. In the course of conversation after dinner, in the cabin of that ship, the former inquired of the latter, if he had seen any of their old shipmates lately; to which he replied, "None but Cecil, and he declines sailing with you again."

"Why?" rejoined Stackpole.

"Because, he says you draw too long a bow for him."

In April, 1814, on the arrival of the Statira in Jamaica, Cecil (then lieutenant of the *Argo* in that port) received a message from Captain Stackpole, through Lieutenant White, demanding an apology for the above expression. Three years having elapsed since Cecil had seen the mid in question, he was greatly astonished, but, having naturally a retentive memory, recollected the circumstance.

Feeling that some explanation was due, he hesitated not to

go on board the *Statira* to make the *amende honorable*; when Captain Stackpole, in no very conciliating tone, demanded a written apology. Cecil expressed his readiness to apportion the reparation to the supposed insult, though no insult was intended; but as the offence was verbal, he considered the apology should also be verbal. Captain Stackpole, however, thought differently, and peremptorily insisted on a written apology, or a meeting the following morning. To which Cecil replied, "In that case I must consult my friends," and retired,

Cecil was no duellist, and his conduct towards Gordon proved that "he bore no malice or hatred in his heart;" that he would not wilfully insult any man, nor would he wantonly sport with human life; he had too nice a sense of right and wrong, of good and evil, not to abhor this abominable, this wicked breach of the laws of God and man. If ever a palliation can be offered, it is in cases of positive self-defence, such as this was; for he knew (in those days) that he would be stigmatized as a coward, and become a jest and a bye-word in the service, if he refused to meet this reputed duellist, "who could knock off a fowl's head with a pistol at twelve paces." To any other officer in the service, he would willingly have given the written apology, but to Captain Stackpole it was impossible. With such a sensitive mind, therefore, there was no alternative but the field; to the field they went—and Stackpole fell.

Alas! who can paint the deep remorse, the mental agony, with which Cecil was overwhelmed at seeing his lifeless foe prostrate on the earth—his very soul melted within him.

Even callous minds would experience a transient regret, but with the keen, the acute sensibility of the highly-gifted Cecil, it was a deadly sting which pierced him to the heart.

In truth, few, very few knew his real character. Adorned with many Christian qualities modestly concealed—endued with an unostentatious heroism rarely surpassed—enriched with a mild and forgiving temper seldom equalled—he was unassuming, frank, and generous; sincere, grateful, and benevolent; energetic, bold, and resolute; a warm friend of refined feeling, and delicately sensitive of honour. In a word, if ever in frail mortality all the virtues were combined, they may be said to have found a kindred dwelling in the lofty soul of Cecil.

Shortly after this melancholy event he was promoted to the rank of commander, but worldly honours had no longer any charms for one who felt that he had slain his fellow-creature; he mourned, he repined in silence; till, at length, inconsolable and unable to bear up against the poignant anguish of this deep affliction, he fell a disconsolate victim to his own sensibility.

Viewing this digression as an offering of respect to the memory of a departed friend, I will now resume the narrative, and observe, that negotiations for exchange of prisoners were frequently attempted by our government, but the acknowledging the *détenus* as legitimate prisoners of war had long been a stumbling-block. At length, however, the humanity of ministers got the better of their prejudices, and they agreed to an exchange, thus tacitly admitting the justice of their detention. But this reluctant concession came too late—the number of French prisoners in England had accumulated to such an enormous amount, that a few hundreds were no longer a consideration; and the French government (after various fruitless propositions on both sides) demanded a general exchange, regardless of rank or numbers; but the giving about five for one, at a period when Buonaparte began to feel the want of men, was too disproportionate to be acceded to; so that these unfortunate individuals seemed doomed to hopeless, endless imprisonment, unwilling victims to the *entêtement* of arbitrary power.

This cruel state of affairs naturally produced extraordinary efforts for relief, and was in fact the cause of the violation of parole which latterly took place—this again produced the decree, which condemned to the gallies all those retaken under such circumstances; bat there was no justice in the discrimination of these cases, for Buonaparte caused a list of all who escaped to be published, representing them as having broken parole—in which list I had the honour to be included, but of the truth or falsehood of this accusation, I leave the reader to judge by the sequel.

Wirion being, as before stated, general-in-chief over the prisoners of war, knew that he should reside at the depôt of officers, wherever that depôt should be; to gratify his spleen, therefore, against the inhabitants of Verdun, with whom he had long been at spiteful variance, he applied to the minister of war, to remove it to Metz; but in this he failed, and the cause of the failure is perhaps worth noticing, as in keeping with Buonaparte's general policy. At the time that Wirion forwarded his application, it was backed by a corresponding one from the inhabitants of Metz, who, in addition to other claims, alleged that the town was more convenient for prisoners than Verdun, as being nearly double the size, and containing treble the number of inhabitants. When these applications were made known to Buonaparte, he referred to his memorandums, and then burst out with—

"Tell them it is a lie, for in my notes on population, Metz is but a village compared to Verdun; Verdun shall keep the prisoners."

This enigma is thus explained. When the prefects and mayors throughout France were ordered to obtain signatures in favour of creating Buonaparte Emperor, the Mayor of Metz returned only twelve names, with an excuse for not being able to obtain more. The Mayor of Verdun, somewhat more cunning, went from house to house, procured as many signatures as he could, and added the names of nearly all the remaining housekeepers, as unable to write, or some other excuse. Thus, in the eyes of Buonaparte, "Metz was but a village compared to Verdun."

Wirion, finding he could not succeed in removing the depot, for a season contented himself with reducing it, and sending to other places all new arrivals, who were not entitled to the rank of officers.

He also now punished most offences with banishment to Bitche, or other depots; although it would at first sight appear, that he was thereby depriving himself of new subjects, upon whom he could more easily practise his *escroqueries*, yet the return to head-quarters always furnished an excuse for exacting fifty crowns, under pretence of defraying the expenses of escort, which in some measure remunerated him for the deficiencies occasioned by this new system.

Things were going on in this manner, when a circumstance occurred, which gave a turn to our destiny, and eventually caused our removal from this scene of dissipation, extortion, roguery, and vice.

In July, 1808, three midshipmen (I blush to state it) were taken in the very act of violating parole: this afforded Wirion an opportunity of representing the whole class, to the minister of war, as contumacious and refractory. He further assured his Excellency, that nothing but extreme rigour and close confinement, could insure the persons of these *très mauvais sujets*, and that Verdun was inadequate to their security. To the joy of some few, besides the peculating general, the result was an order for the whole class to be removed.

Accordingly, on the 7th of August, on going to the afternoon *appel*, we were arrested, to the number of one hundred and forty-two, and sent to the citadel. Although we felt somewhat disconcerted at this sudden and unexpected movement, the natives were still more alarmed. It was natural to suppose, that among so large a number, there were some few in arrears with the tradespeople, who flocked to the gates of the citadel to obtain, if possible, payment, or some security; and it is difficult to say, whether they were more enraged against the general, or against the poor unfortunate mids, who were deprived of all means of making any arrangements, by an order of non-intercourse, which was strictly enforced,

The previous occurrence of similar events, though on a minor scale as to numbers, warned us to prepare for an early departure, but not a word to that effect escaped the commanding-officer, until late at night. Besides the usual inmates of St. Vannes, that monastery was now crammed with such motley groups of gamblers quarrelling, debtors exulting, and Romeos despairing, that the scene was truly entertaining; particularly to those who, having nothing to regret, were looking forward for an opportunity of proving, that parole alone was the bond which had enchained them for so many years.

We were all indiscriminately huddled together in the different apartments of the convent, upon the planks, for the night, and at dawn of day the drum summoned us to muster. All those who were to depart, were drawn up in two ranks; one of seventy-three, destined for Valenciennes and Givet, the other of sixty-nine (most of whom were masters of merchant vessels), destined for Sarre Louis and other depôts, to the eastward. The northern expedition being ready, we were placed two by two, upon bundles of straw, in five wagons, and set out, escorted by the greater part of the horse *gendarmerie* of the district, aided by infantry.

No sooner had we cleared the suburbs, than they assumed a more regular order; four horse *gendarmes* formed the van, and four the rearguard; one on each side of every wagon, and twenty foot soldiers in files, with others in each carriage, made up the escort, the commander bringing up the rear upon his black charger. Whenever the road passed by a wood, which frequently occurred, we were halted, to give the infantry time to occupy its skirts; two gendarmes on each side were posted midway; whilst the rest occasionally displayed their pistols, somewhat ostentatiously, by way of intimidation.

I have been thus minute in detailing the strength and manner of the escort, not only to contrast it with similar detachments in England, where twice the number of French prisoners, with infinitely greater facilities of escape, might be safely entrusted to the care of a serjeant's guard; but also to shew how fully persuaded Wirion was, that some of us would make the attempt.

My most intimate friend and brother mid, Moyses, was of the party, and we had agreed to avail ourselves of the first opportunity to decamp; this, however, appeared almost hopeless, if there should prove no relaxation in the system they had adopted. In the; evening, we arrived at Stenay, having travelled about twenty miles.

Upon halting, we were mustered in two divisions, and shut up in two public-houses; one division, in the lower part of the town, to which the younger and least suspicious were conducted; the other, in a building by itself on the roadside. Particular care was taken to surround both houses, besides placing sentinels at the doors, and in the rooms, so that nothing could be done without considerable danger of discovery. Moyses and myself, nevertheless, continued to make several preparations; by pretending fatigue, we obtained leave to go to bed, and were alone for some time, although repeatedly visited by the *gendarmes*, who, when dinner was announced, were kept in good humour, by being invited to partake of it. We endeavoured to tempt them to a free use of the bottle, but French soldiers are not generally addicted to the destructive vice of drunkenness.

Towards nine p. m. the party lay down on the floor to rest. Moyses and I took our stations in a corner by the window, under which a sentinel was placed, whose turnings were to be watched about eleven, and when his back should be towards the window, Wetherly (a brother mid) was to lower us down with towels tied together. If discovered, the sentinel was to be instantly knocked down; we were to make for the river, distant only a few hundred yards, swim across, and gain the woods: in case of success thus far, it was our intention to have proceeded to those in the vicinity of Verdun, and there wait the assistance of a friend, who was to furnish us with the necessaries for travelling through Germany, to the gulf of Venice.

About ten, the guard was relieved, and we were ordered into a large lighted room, there to lie on the floor, with the *gendarmes* forming nearly a circle around us, the windows barred in, and doors bolted. This unexpected precaution totally frustrated our plans; at daylight we were again assembled in the wagons, and continued our journey, escorted as before.

Nothing particular attracted our attention, our thoughts being chiefly occupied in meditating plans of escape, as circumstances might favour.

"Hope springs eternal in the human breast."

And so actively alive were we to every dawn which beamed on the imagination, that each wood, each copse, which rose to view as we advanced, we fancied invited us to its protection. It was our intention to take the first opportunity, in passing a wood, through which our road sometimes led, to leap from the wagon, and trust to our heels, and its shelter, for security. To this end, we had taken our station in the front of one, with our knapsacks (containing a few articles necessary for a march) on our backs. On approaching a wood, a *gendarme* observed, with a very significant expression of countenance;—

"Messieurs, il me semble que vous vous trouverez plus à votre aise sans l'havresac au dos."[8]

It was evident from this observation, that our purpose was suspected, and that we were narrowly watched. On gaining a hill, we gradually opened upon a rich plain, watered by the Meuse, on the borders of which stands the town of Sedan, having a citadel, with ramparts in a most dilapidated state, which we viewed with secret pleasure, for there appeared but little difficulty in getting clear of the town, if we could but elude the vigilance of the guard, and understanding that here our quarters for the night had been ordered, we were the more elated.

Our march into the town was attended by a numerous rabble of ragged wanderers, and instead of being conducted to prison, as expected, we were halted at a public-house; on reconnoitring the premises, a closet window was discovered, through which we could get upon the roof, and by the aid of a line, let ourselves down into the river, and swim over.

Scarcely were our arrangements made, when we were surprised by the word to muster, again ordered into the wagons, and proceeded on our journey. We were not, however, less firm in the determination to avail ourselves of the first opportunity of making an attempt at liberty; but the cat-like vigilance of the guard, seemed to render escape totally impracticable.

---

8. Gentlemen, I think you would be more at your ease without your knapsacks on your backs.

On reaching Meziers, about eight p.m., we were received at the gates by a strong reinforcement of foot soldiers, and but for the precaution of forming double files on each side, might have had an opportunity of mingling with the mob assembled in the streets. They, however, lodged us safely in the prison, and when secured by bars and bolts, the jailor informed us the morrow would be a *jour de repos*: nothing could be done that night; some, in consideration of a *douceur*, were permitted to occupy the jailor's private apartment. In the morning, we had the range of the prison, and discovered that the only way by which we could possibly escape, was by scaling the wall of the yard, which was about twenty feet in height; this, however, could not be done without a ladder, a grapnel and line, or the assistance of three or four to stand against the wall upon each other's shoulders.

Moyses and myself, were, nevertheless, determined to run any risk, knowing we were to be separated the next day, and there being no one of our party in whom I had at that time so much confidence as my friend; indeed, I felt convinced, that if the night passed without success, I should be doomed to wander alone through dark and desolate tracts, in dreary woods, hunted by all; for I was resolutely bent upon liberty.

Parole had, hitherto, tended, in some measure, to reconcile me to captivity, but being now deprived of that honourable confidence, and feeling my pride wounded, at the oppressive act of punishing the innocent for the guilty, no obstacle could avert my intention of finally executing, what I now felt a duty; and it was cheering to find, that in these feelings, my friend most cordially participated.

His intense anxiety in watching, his firm and resolute demeanour, his readiness in finding a remedy for every new obstacle as it arose, not only excited in me new vigour, but evinced the ardour with which he would have rushed into every danger, if it afforded but a hope of success.

Having arranged our plans; it was determined, in order to avoid whispering, that only one should be entrusted with the secret, until the hour of trial; then, if appearances augured well, others were to be requested to assist. In the afternoon, we were mustered, and separated into two divisions, one bound to Valenciennes, the other to Givet.

About nine, in order to reconnoitre, we obtained permission to go into the yard, whither we were attended by a guard but, finding there, two large dogs running loose, escape was impossible. We felt severely the disappointment of this last hope of decamping together. The jailor, in a jocose way, inquired if the dogs were asleep; he was not, however, so austere, as some of his profession, for although he knew well the use of a map, he hesitated not to sell us one, apparently indifferent to our escape, provided it did not take place from his custody.

We laid ourselves down to rest, encouraged by mutual consolation, when each felt determined, and hoped for the first opportunity of proving the sincerity of a friendship, formed and matured in adversity.

In the morning, the Givet division, having been mustered in the wagons, departed. The party for Valenciennes soon after followed, with a reduced escort, who observed the usual precautions. Being bow left to my own reflections,

"I weighed the danger with the doubtful hope;"

and, without plunging headlong into extremes, resolved, should a favourable opportunity offer, upon following up the former plan—jumping out of the wagon, and bolting into a wood; but the unabated vigilance of the guard rendered it impossible. In the evening, we arrived at Hirson, and the following day at Avesnes. Here I was permitted to go to the military hospital, under an escort, to visit some English seamen, who had been wounded in endeavouring to escape from Arras, and gave them a subscription raised amongst ourselves.

This day, the guard being relieved, we were entrusted to the care of a *Marèchal de logis*, who, entertaining the most liberal opinions of the character of British officers, immediately placed us on parole, and took us to an inn, where we slept. In the morning he selected eight, of whom I was one, and gave us permission to take the diligence to Valenciennes; adding—"Gentlemen, I rely upon your honour."

Now, severity would have been more acceptable than this act of politic kindness; but to have declined the offer, would have exposed my intentions and drawn upon me the accumulated vigilance of the whole guard. This method evinced the impolicy of harsh measures, and insured the safety of eight of the mids.

We set out in the diligence, with one *gendarme*, the mere formality of a guard, and passing through a village met four English seamen, with scarcely a rag to cover them, strongly guarded, chained to each other by the neck, and handcuffed.

They told us, that having escaped from Arras; they had gained the coast, seized a vessel, and put to sea. After beating about for several days in a gale of wind, and splitting all their sails, they were blown back, wrecked on the coast, and, on being retaken, were shamefully treated by the *gendarmes*.

We made a subscription for them, and the poor fellows, with hearts of oak, not to be subdued, gave us three cheers, adding—"Never mind, gentlemen, we'll catch 'em again off Trafalgar, some of these days."

Passing through Quesnoy and Landrecy, we arrived at Valenciennes, about three p. m. August the 17th, 1808. Being soon afterwards joined by the rest of the party, we were conducted with great form to the citadel; there to take up our abode with about fourteen hundred men, who occupied the barracks. A small house, divided into six apartments, each containing three or four beds, was, however, appropriated to the mids; here it was intended we should exist during the war and no distinction whatever was to be made between us *très mauvais sujets*, and the seamen, except the permission of walking on the rampart fronting the town.

Colonel Du Croix Aubert commanded the depôt. It was soon understood, that he would rigidly adhere to his instructions; exercise no tyranny; grant no favours; be guilty of no extortions; but devote his whole time and talent to the security of his important charge. I did not, therefore, indulge in any vain hope of change in our enviable situation, but immediately began to reconnoitre, in order to form plans of escape.

That part of the citadel in which the men were allowed to walk, and which might be termed their play-ground, occupied about an acre; in this confined spot, fourteen hundred men were mustered three times a day, and no one permitted to go out, but under escort. [9]

On the arrival of the mids, the number of sentinels was considerably augmented, and strict orders issued to watch them. From the citadel, escape appeared impossible, it being surrounded with ditches, containing about six feet of mud, on the surface of which was not more than a foot of water: so that swimming was deemed impracticable. In this part of the fortress, which the prisoners termed the lower citadel, there are two gates—the northern, leading to the upper citadel, and the southern, to the town: at each, was a strong guard.

Through the western rampart is a sally-port, which leads into an outwork, thence into a garden, forming a triangle of about half an acre, at the extreme point of which, the Escaut branches off in two streams, the canal passing between the citadel and ravelin. Through this sally-port it was my intention to make an attempt, that appearing the weakest point. I meant to swim across the river, and take my clothed in an umbrella prepared for the occasion. I once tried the efficacy of this plan before many people at Verdun, which drew upon me the displeasure of the police, attended by an order not to repeat my experiments. [10]

---

9. It had been the custom for about two years, to allow one-third of the whole to go into the town to work, on condition of each paying ten *sols* per day to the commandant, whose name I have forgotten; certainly not Du Croix Aubert. Fearing this disgraceful practice might sometime be exposed, he reduced it one half, till, at length, it was entirely abolished by the pretended discovery of the government, who superseded him in this lucrative command, after having permitted him to fill his coffers with nearly six thousand pounds.

10. A strong oil-skin umbrella may be made to float a heavy weight, by first nibbing the seams inside and out with a preparation of bees-wax and tallow; then place it inverted in the water, and stow the clothes carefully round, so that it be fairly equipoised; a swimmer with a line in his teeth can thus tow a tolerable load across a stream, and also another person, who cannot swim, provided he holds on steadily by the ferule at arm's length.

Some few days elapsed before I ventured to communicate these intentions to any one, when I broached the subject to a friend and brother mid, named Ricketts, who readily entered into my views, and was willing to assist me in any way, but from the most honourable motives, declined joining. From the difficulty of getting out of the fort without aid, I hesitated at going alone, and mentioned it to a messmate, named Cadell, who also declined; I then sounded several other midshipmen without success.

In this state of suspense, day after day elapsed, till the 4th of September, when I applied to one whose name was Hunter, he approved of my plans, and appeared gratified that I had selected him as a companion. Shortly afterwards it was agreed, that we should start on the 14th, intending, by means of picklocks, to get through the sally-port; and I was the more sanguine of success, from the circumstance of there being no sentinel at that door.

At length the 14th arrived, everything wearing a favourable aspect, the hour of ten was appointed for the attempt. About four p. m. Hunter, to my surprise and vexation, signified his determination to postpone it until the spring, urging that, from the season of the year, he foresaw innumerable difficulties, and deemed success impossible. In this distress, I became almost frantic, for from so untimely and unexpected secession, I doubted in whom to confide.

My brother officers getting intimation of my intentions, whispered it about from one to another, till it became a topic of general conversation; at length it reached the ears of the police, and, in consequence of this, I was so closely watched, that all my prospects, for the present, were blasted.

The only way to remove these suspicions was perfect tranquillity for some time; and to divert public attention, I sent for my clothes and dogs, which had been left at Verdun, to avoid encumbrance on the road to Valenciennes. It should be observed, that a sentinel was now placed at the before-mentioned sally port, and stricter orders issued throughout the depôt.

The midshipmen began to manifest much impatience at the

continuance of their *durance vile*, and, after several fruitless applications to the commandant, drew up a letter to the minister of war, requesting restoration, to parole; one sentence of which insured a flat denial, as it plainly intimated that a refusal would be attended with escape; it ran to this effect—

"Such is the character of the British officer, that his *parole d' honneur* will better secure his person, than locks, bolts, and fortresses."

A few days afterwards, I was delighted to learn, that the minister's answer was confined to a simple negative. On the arrival of my clothes and dogs from Verdun, I pretended to think of little else, except the study of Spanish; and these being the usual subjects of my conversation, the general suspicion gradually subsided, till no one but Ricketts and Cadell entertained an idea of the many schemes I was plotting with a view to departure.

I kept up a correspondence, *per* post, with my friend Moyses, and several others in Verdun, all of whom were instructed to declaim against escape, as being extremely dangerous, and disapproved of by the senior officers; this was done, because all our letters were opened, and it tended to deceive the police. It was my wish, that Moyses should make interest to be sent to Valenciennes; such removals being sometimes effected through the application of our own officers.

Finding there was no probability of a junction, and all suspicion being at length removed, I again commenced sounding those around me, when an opening was found to make a proposal to a brother mid, named Rochfort; he came into it immediately, the strictest secrecy was observed, and, to avoid suspicion, we determined to be seldom seen together. He was well calculated for the adventure, as he was known to be a good seaman, endowed with great bodily strength, and what was still more necessary, possessed of firmness of mind; my only fear was of rashness on his part, for to afford a chance of success in such an enterprise, it was of the utmost importance that courage, strength, and prudence should go hand in hand.

With the assistance of Ricketts and Cadell, our preparations were completed, and the 15th of October, was fixed for departure. I was the more anxious to carry our plans into execution, so soon as matured, because the commandant with unremitting and admirable diligence daily visited the citadel; issued stricter regulations for the safe custody of the prisoners; and as frequently changed the posts of the sentinels, demanding a corresponding change on our part; at length, it was ordered, that anyone, who should be seen in the night, without a lantern, whether English or French, should be instantly fired at, and, in the event of a *gendarme's* light being accidentally extinguished, while visiting the sentinels, which was done every half hour, he was to be constantly repeating—"*Gendarme* without light," until he reached the guard room. Besides these precautions, there were regular patrols: the difficulty and danger of escape had, therefore, considerably increased, and it became necessary, that our caution should keep pace with their vigilance.

There still being a sentinel at the sally-port, my first plan was changed to that of getting into the upper citadel, which could only be effected by creeping upon the parapet above the north-gate, letting ourselves down upon the bridge, over the canal, and passing through the ravelin; but being unacquainted with those parts of the fortification, we intended to risk all, and trust to Providence for deliverance.

This plan, did not bear the stamp of prudence, but what could we do better? It was, in fact, our only resource. The subject was discussed temperately and deliberately. Notwithstanding a sentry box was placed directly over the north gate, it was evident that that was the only practicable point. These obstacles, however, instead of damping our hopes, only gave new life to an energy, which rose with the emergency; indeed, we persuaded ourselves, that the very precautions taken, would ultimately facilitate our elopement; for the *gendarmes*, judging, that from the number of night sentinels, we should deem it impracticable, would, in the course of time, be so lulled into security, as to relax, and become more careless than if they were less numerous.

By the friendly aid of Mr. M'Intosh, a *détenu*, residing in the town, we procured provisions, and a map of the northern department, as also several other necessaries, for such an expedition. The only thing now wanting was rope, this we obtained by purchasing skipping-lines of the boys, which was a general amusement amongst them at this season; the bringing such small quantities openly into the citadel, excited no suspicion, and, in order to ascertain the requisite length, I counted the courses of bricks, in the pillars in the inner part of the north gate; which, allowing four to a foot, and five feet to the breast-work, made the height about forty-five feet to the bridge.

Everything being ready, and the day arrived, without any one entertaining the slightest suspicion, I was so fully persuaded of being in England in a few days, that I strutted about the citadel, smiling at every self-sufficient gendarme I met, half inclined to say, jocosely—*Adieu*; for, notwithstanding the multiplied difficulties, mutual confidence made us not only look upon them as trifles, but almost created a wish they were still greater, that the honour of surmounting them might be proportionally conspicuous, and thereby the astonishment and disappointment of the watchful commandant be the more excited; for he would rather have lost ten seamen, than one of those *très-mauvais sujets*.

Ricketts, who watched my proceedings with the anxious eye of friendship, viewed with more coolness the chances of failure and success, in all their bearings, and being aware that we were still ignorant of the difficulties to be encountered, in our progress to the upper citadel, did not appear so sanguine as ourselves. These difficulties, however, scarcely arrested our attention; for we were so wrapped up in the enchanting idea of sweet liberty, the glorious prospect of proving the inefficacy of "locks, bolts, and fortresses," and the still stronger incentive of again wearing arms in the service of our country, that no obstacle could damp our ardour.

About five p. m., on the day fixed for our departure, I was walking with Ricketts, and discussing the proposed plans, which were then ripe for execution, when Cadell came up, and told us that Rochfort had just been seized with headache and fever, so violent as to require his being immediately put to bed. This I could scarcely credit, until made an eye-witness of the fact. Struck with astonishment, I gazed on the sufferer, and, scarcely able to ask a question, stole into the yard, absorbed in thought and perplexity; not cherishing the faintest hope of finding another in the citadel to join with me. The fact was, that from my having been before suspected, and publicly denounced, and likewise from my being aware of the extent to which "espionage" was practised in the fort, I was backward in introducing the subject to several, who have since proved by their conduct that they would readily have accompanied me. I wandered about for some time, reflecting on this extraordinary occurrence, little suspicious of what was afterwards developed, that, from our total ignorance of the impediments in passing into the upper citadel, failure, and its attendant consequences, must have been the result of trial at this time.

My mind, however, was not to be diverted from the object in view, and, no sooner had I roused myself from the effect of this disheartening event, than I began to meditate new schemes, for I was resolved on the attempt *coute qui coute*; but hesitated, whether to await Rochfort's recovery, or to look out for another companion.

Day after day passed in this state of suspense; when, finding no amendment in his health, he was liberal enough to advise my seeking a helpmate amongst the seamen. He became so reduced by illness, that even, if he should recover, he would not dare to risk exposure to night chills, for a considerable time; it was, therefore, with extreme reluctance, I abandoned the hope of his company. I then cautiously sounded several of the most steady of the quarter-masters, and petty officers of that class, without success.

Whether they doubted the possibility of escape, or were deterred by the recollection of the barbarous murders at Bitche, I cannot say; for it was known, that when the commandant of that place had gained intimation of an intended attempt, he suffered the fugitives to reach a certain point, where *gendarmes* lurking in ambush were ready to rush in, and murder. Two sailors, named Marshall and Cox, fell victims to this refined system of republican discipline.

A somewhat similar act of cold-blooded atrocity, afterwards occurred at Givet, in the person of Hay ward, a midshipman: this gallant fellow, with his friend, Gale, had broken out of prison, in the face of day, and fled into the country; unfortunately, they were discovered, and the alarm given; two horse *gendarmes* immediately pursued, and overtook them in an open field.

On their approach, Hayward, being unarmed, and seeing escape impossible, stood still, extended his hands, and exclaimed—"*Je me rends*:" but this was too favourable an opportunity to be neglected, for the savage gratification of shedding human blood. Neither the defenceless state of the individual, nor his prompt surrender could deter these merciless miscreants from plunging their swords into his manly chest, and mangling the body in a horrible manner. It was afterwards taken into the prison-yard, stripped naked, and exposed to the view of the prisoners, for the purpose of intimidating others from the like attempt. Gale gave himself up at the same time; and, although he received several severe wounds, they did not prove mortal.[11]

The ingenuity of fourteen hundred men was put to the test, to furnish amusement for the most wearisome hours that can be imagined, and in utter ignorance of their termination, or what was passing in the busy world of strife.

The greater part, by lifeless endless *ennui*, were reduced to such a state of apathy, that they were worn down into mere brute existence; whilst those who had still any energy left, magnified the most trifling occurrence into an important event.

On the 21st of October, being the anniversary of the battle of Trafalgar, almost every window in the citadel was illuminated,

---

11. It will scarcely be credited, that the commandant gave the perpetrators of this courageous exploit a pecuniary reward, with this observation:—"I give you this, for having killed one of them; had you killed both, the reward would have been doubled."

and several transparencies were exhibited in honour of that glorious victory. The repeated and almost incessant cheering of the prisoners, continued for nearly two hours; many of the inhabitants of the town obtained leave to visit the citadel, and appeared to join in the sport with all their characteristic frivolity. About this time, a club was formed in the midshipmen's quarters, which its convivial members designated by the title of "Union." I was invited to become a member, but, as the nature of its amusements did not accord with my habits, it was not until about the 25th of October that I could be prevailed on to join it, and then only with a view of averting any suspicion that might otherwise arise, as to my meditated plans.

One regulation imposed the penalty of drinking a tumbler of brandy, on the refusal to sing a song. As I could do neither, the tide of disapprobation was flowing against me, when, on condition of the remission of my penalty, I engaged, at the following meeting, to sing one that no one had ever heard; that day arrived, my poetical as well as vocal talents were brought into action, and exerted upon the prevailing foibles of every one present.

The song, which was the one alluded to in Miller's work, was received with *éclat* and good humour, and ever afterwards sung by the president, at the opening of the club, so long as it existed. The following Saturday, I was again about to be fined, when I repeated my former engagement, provided we should all be together.

Having, for some time, vainly indulged the hope of finding a companion willing to share my fate, and the winter fast approaching, I became apprehensive of not being able to make the attempt before the ensuing spring.

In the beginning of November, two sailors were sparring in the yard, and so common was this amusement, that it attracted the notice of no one but a stupid conscript of a sentinel, who, fancying they were quarrelling, quitted his post, and commenced a brutal attack on them, with the butt end of his musket: this breach of military discipline, soon collected a mob, and the endeavours of the men to ward off the blows, gave them the appearance of acting offensively.

The guard was called out, when the *gendarmes*, rushing through the mob, cut and slashed on all sides. Whitehurst, whom I mentioned in the early part of this *Narrative*, and I, happening to be there at the time, roused with indignation at such wanton barbarity, also pushed in, in the hope of preventing bloodshed. The *Marèchal de logis*, observing us in the *mêlée*, desired us to send the men to their rooms; upon the order being given, they immediately retired.

This prompt obedience, bearing the appearance of generally acting under our influence, was, no doubt, the cause of our being denounced, as the authors of the disturbance. We were, however, allowed to retire, whilst nine men, who were wounded, were seized as ringleaders; some were put into the *cachot*, and others sent to the hospital.

The next morning, Whitehurst and I were arrested, and conducted to a separate place of confinement, upon the rampart, fronting the town. We were there locked up, with a sentinel at the door, without communication with any one, and ordered to be kept on bread and water. We were secretly informed, that the commandant had forwarded a report to the minister of war, representing us as *chefs de complot*; the punishment of which, by the "Code Napoleon," is death.

Although this did not much trouble us, being conscious of the falsehood of the accusation, yet we judged it right to lay before the commandant a firm and accurate relation of the facts, referring him to the *Marèchal de logis*, for proof of our interference having prevented more bloodshed, and restored tranquillity. This respectful appeal to the justice of the commandant Du Croix Aubert, corroborated by the evidence of the *Marèchal de logis*, succeeded in restoring us to our comrades, and in inducing him to transmit a counter-statement to the minister of war. I mention this circumstance, because it produced a proposition on the part of Whitehurst, to attempt escape, so soon as we could make the necessary preparations.

I eagerly embraced his proposal; and, although I knew that,

from his inexperience in the management of small craft, his assistance could not be great, in the event of getting afloat; I was perfectly convinced of his willingness and resolution. This consideration rendered it necessary, however, to seek a third person, and I sounded five men, separately, in the course of the day; but, so prevalent was the belief of the impossibility of getting out of the fortress, except by bribery, that they all declined.

In this difficulty, I consulted Ricketts, who proposed to introduce the subject again to Hunter. I determined to overlook his forsaking me on the 14th of September, and consented to accept him as a companion, provided we departed in a week; this stipulation being conveyed to him, and our prospects painted in glowing colours, he agreed to join us.

From that moment, he behaved with firmness and cordiality: not an hour was lost in procuring everything needful for the occasion; but before we could fix the precise day, we resolved to obtain some information, respecting the obstacles in our passage to the upper citadel, that being the only way by which we could possibly escape. It was necessary to be very cautious in this particular, and many schemes were suggested.

At length, hearing that that part of the fortifications abounded in wild rabbits, my greyhounds were offered to one of the *gendarmes*, whenever he chose to make use of them. And the fellow mentioned it to the *Marèchal de logi*s, who was equally pleased with the expectation of sport, for they verily believed, that such beautiful English dogs could kill every rabbit they saw. Shortly afterwards, the *gendarme* came, with the keys in his hand, for them; the *Marèchal de logis* waiting at the gate. The dogs, however, had been taught to follow no one but their master, so that their refusing to go, afforded me an opportunity of making an offer to accompany them, which was immediately accepted.

Whitehurst, Hunter, and two or three others, requested to go with us; four other *gendarmes* were ordered to attend, and we went in a tolerably large party. We took different directions round the ramparts, kicking the grass, under pretence of looking for rabbits; few were found, and none killed; but we succeeded in making our observations, and in about an hour returned, fully satisfied of the practicability of escape; though the difficulties we had to encounter were, to scale a wall, to ascend the parapet unseen, to escape the observation of three or four sentinels and the patrols, to descend two ramparts, of about forty-five feet each, to force two large locks; and to get over two draw-bridges. These were not more than we expected, and we, therefore, prepared accordingly.

On our return, we fixed the night of the 15th of November, for the attempt. In the mean time, my friend, M'Intosh, then residing in town, got iron-handles put to a pair of steel boot-hooks, given to me by Craig, which I intended to use as picklocks. The only thing now wanting was another rope, and as that belonging to the well in the midshipmen's yard was (from decay) not trustworthy, in the night we hacked several of the heart-yarns, so that the first time it was used in the morning it broke. A subscription was made by the mids, and a new one applied for; by these means, we had, at command, about thirty-six feet, in addition to what our friends had before purchased of the boys. Everything was now prepared; the spirits and provisions in the knapsacks were concealed in the dog-kennel.

On the 14th, Whitehurst communicated the secret to a young mid, named Mansell, who immediately proposed to join, and my consent was requested; but I strongly objected, under the impression of his being unable to endure the privations and hardships to which we might probably be exposed: by the persuasion of Ricketts and Cadell, however, I at last consented.

At length the time arrived which I had so ardently desired, and the feelings of delight with which I hailed it, were such as allowed me to anticipate the happiest results. The thought of having lost so many years from the service of my country, during an active war, had frequently embittered hours which would otherwise have been cheerful and merry, and now proved a stimulant to perseverance, exceeded only by that which arose from the desire I felt, to impress upon the minds of Frenchmen, the inefficacy of vigilance and severity to enchain a British officer, when compared with that milder, and more certain mode of securing his person—"confiding in his honour."

As the sun declined, our excitement increased. Our plans had been conducted with such, profound secrecy, that only our most confidential friends entertained the slightest suspicion of our intention. At the usual hour we retired to rest; at half-past eleven we arose, and, in preparation for our departure, went into the midshipmen's little yard, unspliced the well-rope, and returned to the apartment.

Desirous of bidding *adieu* to our messmates, the six [12], who slept in the room were awakened. On seeing the manner in which we were equipped, the rope slung over the shoulder, the knapsacks, the implements, and the laugh each one was endeavouring to stifle, they were so confused, that they could not, for the moment, comprehend why we were thus attired. When told that we intended being in England in ten days, they exclaimed, "impossible;" and argued against the attempt, as nothing better than the effect of insanity, insisting, that we were obstinately running, with our eyes open, into the very mouth of destruction. But, as such remarks, if listened to, might only have tended to create indecision, we shook hands, and said, Good night

When about to depart, Cadell observed, we had better wait a few minutes, as it was then very star-light, and nearly a calm. His advice was attended to, and we impatiently waited the passing of a cloud, in the hope of its increasing the obscurity; but the clouds dispersed, the wind died away, and nothing disturbed the silence of the night but the watch-calls of the sentinels, and the occasional footsteps of the patrols. This anxious state of suspense continued until two o'clock, when we again rose to depart, but were prevented by the kind interference of our friends, who insisted on our waiting a little longer, arguing, that as I had met with so many disappointments, and had so repeatedly avowed my intention to act prudently, we ought to wait, even till the morrow-night, if necessary.

"What folly," continued Ricketts, "to blast all your prospects,

---

12. Messrs. Sutton, Hamilton, Cadell, Greig, Bisset, and Wetherly.

by false notions of honour;" but the idea of flinching at this crisis, was so repugnant to my feelings, and so wounding to my pride, that it was with the utmost reluctance, I could consent to postpone the attempt another minute. On reflection, however, I felt the propriety of his remarks, and also that our liberty and lives being, in a great measure, dependent upon my discretion, it behoved me not to allow my judgement to be influenced by the opinions of the illiberal or hot-headed, who, I feared, would attribute our delay to other causes, than the real one; however, that mattered little; patient and persevering, we anxiously watched the stars, and sensibly alive to everything that could for a moment endanger the confidence reposed in me, by my companions, I listened with attention to their opinions; when, finding them to coincide with my own, and the clock now striking three, we agreed to postpone the attempt, till the following night, and then start about eight p. m.; all present promised secrecy; we replaced the well-rope, returned our knapsacks to the care of the greyhounds, and retired to bed.

The next morning nothing material occurred; the movements, of the preceding night were unsuspected. In the afternoon we amused ourselves with writing a letter to the commandant, in which we thanked him for his civilities, and assured him, that it was the rigid and disgraceful measures of the French government which obliged us to prove the inefficacy of "lock, bolts, and fortresses" and that if he wished to detain British officers, the most effectual method was to put them upon their "honour;" for that alone was the bond which had enchained us for more than five years.

This letter was left with Ricketts to be dropped on the following day near the *corps de garde*. At half-past seven p. m. we assembled, each provided with a clasp-knife and a paper of fine pepper, upon which we placed our chief dependence; for, in case of being closely attacked, we intended to throw a handful into the eyes of the assailants, and then to retreat.

The plan was, that Hunter and myself were to depart first, fix the rope, and open the opposing doors; a quarter of an hour afterwards, Whitehurst and Mansell were to follow: by these means we diminished the risk attendant on so large a body as four moving together, and secured the advantage of each depending more upon his own care; for if Hunter and myself were shot in the advance, the other two would remain in safety, and if, on the contrary, they were discovered, we hoped to have time during the alarm to gain the country. Our intentions were to march to the sea-side, and range the coast to Breskins, in the island of Cadsand, opposite Flushing; and if means of getting afloat were not found before arriving at that place, we proposed to embark in the passage-boat for Flushing, and, about mid-channel, rise and seize the vessel.

It was now blowing very fresh, and was so dark and cloudy, that not a star could be seen; the leaves were falling in abundance, and as they were blown over the stones, kept up a constant rustling noise, which was particularly favourable to the enterprise; indeed, things wore so promising an appearance, that we resolved to take leave of a few other of our brother officers: accordingly Messrs, Halford, Rochfort, Wright, Miller, Mahony, Robinson, and two others were invited; to these I detailed our exact situation, the difficulties we had to contend with, and the means of surmounting them, reminded them of our letter to the commandant of last month, and the glory of putting our threats into execution in spite of his increased vigilance, read the one we had that afternoon written, and proposed that any of them should follow that chose, but with this stipulation, that they allowed four hours to elapse before they made the attempt. Upon which, it being a quarter past eight, Hunter and I, with woollen socks over our shoes, that our footsteps might not be heard, and each having a rope, a small poker or a stake, and knapsack, took leave of our friends and departed.

We first went into the back yard, and, assisted by Rochfort, who was now convalescent, but not sufficiently strong to join the party, got over the wall, passed through the garden and palisades, crossed the road, and climbed silently upon our hands and knees up the bank, at the back of the north guard room, lying perfectly still as the sentinels approached, and as they receded, again advancing, until we reached the parapet over the gateway leading to the upper citadel.

Here the breast-work over which we had to creep, was about five feet high and fourteen thick, and, it being the highest part of the citadel, we were in danger of being seen by several sentinels below; but, fortunately, the cold bleak wind induced some of them to take shelter in their boxes. With the utmost precaution we crept upon the summit, and down the breast-work towards the outer edge of the rampart, when the sentinel made his quarter-hourly cry of "*Sentinelle prenez garde à vous*," similar to our "All's well;" this, though it created for a moment rather an unpleasant sensation, convinced me that we had reached thus far unobserved.

I then forced the poker into the earth, and, by rising and falling with nearly my whole weight, hammered it down with my chest; about two feet behind, I did the same with the stake, then slipped the eye of the well-rope over the head of the poker, and fastened a small line from the upper part of the poker to the lower part of the stake (see fig. 1.): this done, we gently let the rope down through one of the grooves in the rampart, which receives a beam of the draw-bridge when up. I then cautiously descended this half chimney, as it were, by the rope; when I had reached about two-thirds of the way down, part of a brick fell, struck against the side and rebounded against my chest, this I luckily caught between my knees and carried down without noise.

I crossed the bridge, and waited for Hunter, who descended with equal care and silence. We then entered the ravelin, proceeded through the arched passage which forms an obtuse angle with a massive door leading to the upper citadel, and with my picklock endeavoured to open it; but not finding the bolt yield with gentle pressure, I added the other hand, and gradually increased the force until by exerting my whole strength something broke. I then tried to file the catch of the bolt, but that being cast iron the file made no impression; we then endeavoured to cut away the stone in the wall which receives the bolt, but that was fortified with a bar of

GAURDING THE CITADEL

iron, so that it was impracticable; the picklocks were again applied, but with no better success. It now appeared complete check-mate (see fig. 2.), and, as the last resource, it was proposed to return to the bridge, slip down the piles, and float along the canal on our backs, there being too little water to swim and too much mud to ford it.

Hunter, with the most deliberate coolness, suggested the getting up the rope again, and attempting some other part of the fortress. In the midst of our consultation, it occurred to me that it would be possible to undermine the gate: this plan was no sooner proposed than commenced, but having no other implements than our pocket-knives, some time elapsed before we could indulge any reasonable hopes of success; the pavement-stones under the door were about ten inches square, and so closely bound together, that it was a most difficult and tedious process. About a quarter of an hour had been thus employed, when we were alarmed by a sudden noise, similar to the distant report of a gun, echoing in tremulous reverberations through the arched passage, and as the sound became fainter, it resembled the cautious opening of the great gate, creating a belief that we were discovered. We jumped up, drew back towards the bridge, intending, if possible, to steal past the gendarmes, and slip down the piles into the canal, but the noise subsiding we stood still, fancying we heard the footsteps of a body of men.

The recollection of the barbarous murders at Bitche on a similar occasion, instantly presented itself to my sensitive imagination; it is impossible to describe the conflicting sensations which rushed upon my mind during this awful pause. Fully impressed with the conviction of discovery and of falling immediate victims to the merciless rage of ferocious blood-hounds, in breathless anxiety I stood and listened, with my knife in savage grasp, waiting the dreadful issue, when suddenly I felt a glow flush through my veins, which hurried me on with the desperate determination to succeed or make a sacrifice of life in the attempt.

We had scarcely reached the turning when footsteps were

Undermining the Gate in the Ravelin at Valenciennes

again heard; and in a whispering tone, "Boys." This welcome sound created so sudden a transition from desperation to serenity, from despair to so pleasing a conviction of success, that in an instant, all was hope and joy. Reinforced by our two friends, we again returned to our work of mining, with as much cheerfulness and confidence as though already embarked for England.

They told us the noise was occasioned by the fall of a knapsack, which Mansell, unable to carry down the rope, had given to Whitehurst, from whom it slipped, and falling upon a hollow sounding bridge, between two lofty ramparts, echoed through the arched passage with sufficient effect to excite alarm.

Whitehurst, with much presence of mind, stood perfectly still when he landed on the bridge, and heard the sentinel walk up to the door on the inside, and stand still also; at this time, they were not more than four feet from each other, and, had the sentinel stood listening a minute longer, he must have heard Mansell land.

Three of us continued mining until half-past ten, when the first stone was raised, and in twenty minutes the second; about eleven, the hole was large enough to allow us to creep under the door. The draw-bridge was up; there was, however, sufficient space between it and the door, to allow us to climb up, and the draw-bridge being square, there was, of course, an opening under the arch (see fig. 3.): through this opening we crept, lowered ourselves down by the second rope, which was passed round the chain of the bridge, and keeping both parts in our hands, landed on the *guarde fous*.[13]

Had these bars been taken away, escape would have been impossible; there being not sufficient rope for descending into the ditch. By keeping both parts of it in our hands, the last man was enabled to bring it away; otherwise four ropes would have been necessary (see fig. 3.)

We then proceeded through another arched passage, with the intention of undermining the second door, but, to our great sur-

---

13. The *guarde fous* are two iron bars, one above the other, suspended by chains on each side of the bridge, when down, serving the purpose of hand-rails.

prise and joy, we found the *gendarmes* had neglected to lock it. The draw-bridge was up; this, however, detained us but a short time: we got over, crossed the ditch upon the *guarde fous*, as before, and landed in the upper citadel.

We proceeded to the north-east curtain, fixed the stake and fastened the rope upon the breast-work for the fourth descent.

As I was getting down, with my chest against the edge of the parapet, the stake grave way. Whitehurst, who was sitting by it, snatched hold of the rope, and Mansell, of his coat, whilst I endeavoured to grasp the grass, by which I was saved from a fall of about fifty feet. Fortunately there was a solitary tree in the citadel; from this a second stake was cut, and the rope doubly secured as before.

We all got down safe with our knapsacks, except Whitehurst, who, when about two-thirds of the way, from placing his feet against the rampart, and not letting them slip so fast as his hands, got himself in nearly a horizontal position; seeing his danger, I seized the rope, and placed myself in rather an inclined posture under him; he fell upon my arm and shoulder with at violent shock; fortunately neither of us were hurt: but it is somewhat remarkable, that within the lapse of a few minutes, we preserved each other from probable destruction.

The vivid imagination of the indulgent reader will better depict, than I can describe our feelings at this momentous period; suffice it to say, that we heartily congratulated ourselves upon our providential success, after a perilous and laborious work of three hours and three quarters, and, in the excess of joy, all shook hands.

Having put our knapsacks a little in order, we mounted the glacis, and followed a footpath which led to the eastward. But a few minutes elapsed, when several objects were observed on the ground, which imagination, ever on the alert, metamorphosed into *gendarmes* in ambush; we however marched on, when, to our no small relief, they were discovered to be cattle. Gaining the high road, we passed (two and two, about forty paces apart) through a very long village, and having travelled three or four miles, felt ourselves so excessively thirsty, that we stopped to drink at a ditch; in the act of stooping, a sudden flash of lightning, from the south-ward, so frightened us (supposing it to be the alarm-gun), that, instead of waiting to drink, we ran for nearly half an hour.

We stopped a second time, and were prevented by a second flash, which alarmed us even more than the first, for we could not persuade ourselves it was lightning, though no report was heard. Following up the road in quick march, our attention was suddenly arrested by a drawbridge, which being indicative of a fortified place, we suspected a guard-house to be close at hand, and were at first apprehensive of meeting with a serious impediment; but observing the gates to be open, we concluded that those at the other extremity would be also open, and therefore pushed forward. We drank at the pump in the square, when it was recollected that this was the little town of St. Amand. Directing our course by the north-star, which was occasionally visible, we passed through without seeing a creature.

About an hour afterwards, still continuing a steady pace, four stout fellows rushed out from behind a hedge, and demanded where we were going. Whitehurst and Mansell immediately ran up; and, as we had previously resolved never to be taken by equal numbers, each seized his pepper and his knife in preparation for fight or flight, replying, in a haughty tone of defiance, "What is that to you, be careful how you interrupt military men:" then whispered loud enough for them to hear, "*la bayonette,*" upon which they dropped astern, though they still kept near us: [14] in the course of a quarter of an hour, on turning an angle of the road, we lost sight of them, and continued a rapid march, frequently running, until about five a. m., when we were unexpectedly stopped by the closed gates of a town.

We retraced our steps a short distance, in the hope of discovering some other road, but we could find neither a footpath, nor wood, nor any other place of concealment. We quitted the high road, and drew towards a rising ground, there to wait the dawn

---

14. These men were robbers.

of day, in the hope of retreating to some neighbouring copse; no sooner had laid we ourselves upon the ground, than sleep overcame us.

Our intention was, if no wood could be seen, to go to an adjoining ploughed field, and there scratch a hole in which we could hide ourselves from a distant view; upon awakening from a short slumber, we reconnoitred around, and found our position to be near a fortification; being well acquainted with such places, we approached, in the hope of finding an asylum. At break of day, we descended into the ditch, and found the entrance into the subterraneous works of the covered way nearly all blocked up with ruins and bushes; an opening, however, was made, we crept in, our quarters were established, and the rubbish and bushes replaced in the space of a few minutes.

This most providential and pleasing discovery, added to our many narrow escapes from detection, excited a feeling of gratitude to that omnipotent Being, who in his infinite mercy had thus cast his protecting wings around us.

I have since heard, that the first intimation of our departure at Valenciennes was at dawn of day, when, on opening the north gate, the rope was seen, suspended from the parapet. The roll to muster was instantly beaten, and the alarm given to the neighbouring peasantry by the firing of guns. The midshipmen, on whom suspicion first fell, were hurried into ranks, half-dressed, and when the names of the absentees were called over, someone tauntingly replied, "*Parti pour l'Angleterre.*"—This tone of triumph considerably exasperated the *gendarmes*, and inflamed the zeal of the pursuers; it also might have had some influence in exciting the solicitude of the commandant for our apprehension.

But to give a more adequate idea of the fury of his wrath and disappointment, and also of his determination to recover us, dead or alive, I may add, (as I have since learnt, from a respectable inhabitant who happened to dine in his company a few days after he had received the mids' first application to be restored to parole,) that he treated escape as utterly impossible and hopeless, and unreservedly spoke of the letter as containing a threat—a mere *gasconade*—"*Nous verrons,*" said he, "*si ces blancs-becs peuvent m'échapper.*"

The report of this threat was soon circulated, and when it was really executed, my informant assured me, that no occurrence relating to the prisoners excited a more general sensation; the whole town was in confusion. All the bloody-minded rabble were let loose, with multifarious weapons, and *carte blanche*, to *massacrer* these lawless *très-mauvais sujets* Besides which, 500 of the *garde nationale* were despatched to scour all the woods within five leagues, and an additional reward of 300 *livres* was offered, for the capture of each of us. The reason for limiting the search to that distance, was a belief of the improbability of our having exceeded it, after the arduous task of undermining, &c. The fact was, that in anticipation of all this, we made a desperate effort to reach as far from Valenciennes as we could before dawn of day.

But to proceed:—we were totally unacquainted with the country; an examination of the maps pointed out the place of our retreat to be the fortification of Tournay; the fallen ruins were the bed upon which fatigue and a confidence of security procured us a sound and refreshing sleep. At three p. m. we enjoyed our dinner, notwithstanding the want of beverage, for upon examining the knapsacks, the flasks were found broken. Whitehurst, having lost his hat in descending the first rampart, was occupied in manufacturing a cap from the skirts of his coat.

It rained all the afternoon, and the weather, in the evening, getting worse, we were detained till about ten p. m, when, no prospect of its clearing up presenting itself, we quitted our comfortable abode, walked round the citadel, to the westward, over ploughed ground, until, coming to a turnip field, we regaled ourselves most sumptuously. By eleven, we had rounded the town, and gained the north road.

During the night we passed through several villages, without seeing any one, and, at six a. m. arrived at the suburbs of Courtray, expecting there to find as snug a retreat as the one we had left the preceding evening; but, to our mortification, the town was enclosed with wet ditches, which obliged us to seek safety elsewhere. Observing a farmhouse on the right, our steps were directed towards it, and thence through bye-lanes, until a mansion was discovered; this we approached, in the hope of finding an out-house which would afford us shelter for the day; nothing of the kind could be seen; but, not far distant, a thicket was descried, of about 150 paces square, surrounded by a wet ditch, from fourteen to twenty feet wide.

Here then we determined to repose our wearied limbs, and, it being daylight, not a moment was to be lost: the opposite side of the narrowest part of the ditch was one entire bed of brambles, and, in the midst of these, we were obliged to leap. Hunter, Mansell, and I, got over tolerably well; but when Whitehurst made the attempt, stiff with wet and cold, and the bank giving way from his great weight, he jumped into the water, and it was with some difficulty he could be extricated, and not without being dragged through the brambles, by which he was severely scratched.

We lay down in the centre of this swampy thicket. The rain had continued without intermission from the time of leaving Tournay, and, notwithstanding it somewhat discommoded us, yet we were consoled by the additional security it afforded this little island protected us till near dark, when we walked round it to find the easiest point of egress. From the torrents of rain that had fallen during the day, but which had now ceased, the ditches had become considerably wider, and there was only one opening in the bushes, whence a leap could be made; of this three of us profited, the fourth obtained a passage by the aid of a decayed willow, which overhung the opposite bank.

Courtray being fortified, it was impossible to cross the river Lys at that place; we were, consequently, obliged to go to Deynse, that being an open town. About eight p. m., proceeding over ploughed ground, rendered almost impassable by the heavy rains, to gain the high road, guided by the north-star, and assisted by a strong southern wind, we marched on at a great rate, and, about ten, entered the village of Haerlabeck. Observing a "cabaret," at the north end, Whitehurst here purchased bread and gin, our remaining bread being completely saturated with moisture; this regale re-animated and fortified us against the inclemency of the weather, which it was apprehended might be productive of sickness.

At one a. m., the rain recommenced, and, in such profusion, that it obliged us to retreat to the protection of a neighbouring haystack, where we lay some time, but, finding no chance of fine weather, we resumed our march until five, and then entered a wood about three miles from Deynse; a spot was chosen in the thickest part, where we fenced ourselves with fallen leaves, twigs, and rubbish of about a foot in height.

We lay down in our little redoubt, and slept until day-break, when, finding our position too exposed, from its proximity to a cottage and the main road, we were obliged to quit it, but previously broke up the work. Having penetrated farther into the wood, we concealed ourselves as before; here we remained during the day, listening to the howling of the wind, which rose gradually into a furious storm of driving sleet, rain, and hail; and, such was its violence, that our garments were scarcely felt to be a covering.

We quitted this wood soon after dark, and gained the high road for Deynse. After marching about an hour, and passing several people (Whitehurst and Mansell always preserving their stipulated distance in the rear), we were overtaken by two horse *gendarmes*; but it being exceedingly dark, they took us for conscripts, part of their own escort, for one of them, in a muffled tone, as if fearful of exposing his nose, said, "Make haste, you will be too late for your lodging-tickets;" reply was made that we were fatigued; soon afterwards, the rain increasing, they trotted on, repeating, "Make haste, Make haste."

We were not much flattered by the honour of their company, but not in such danger as one might imagine, for the road was between two woods, with a broad ditch on each side; had they stopped to dismount, we should instantly have jumped over, and run into the wood, where no cavalry could have pursued.

The rain continued to pour heavily, and, having been completely soaked to the skin during many hours, about ten p. m. we held a council of war. Although such consultations have been designated the "bane of enterprise" and considered an effort on the part of the commanding officer to diminish his responsibility in the event of failure, it was not so with us;—for, being without a commander, we consulted upon almost every important measure; the unanimity that prevailed, not only rendered success more certain, but made each bear his own individual privations with cheerfulness, and proved a stimulant to energy, which increased with increasing difficulties and sufferings.

After mature deliberation, it was agreed to enter the town, and reconnoitre the low public houses, in order to purchase provisions; we accordingly marched on, Whitehurst entered one, which he found too full of company, and then a second, in which he saw four stupid looking young men, almost as wet as ourselves. We resolved all to go in, keeping the door at; the elbow in case of necessity; we did so, and, asking for gin, drew round the stove.

From the conversation of these men, it appeared, that a large party of conscripts had arrived that evening, on their road to Ghent, and were billeted about the town this information we immediately turned to account. Our landlord was given to understand we were conscripts, who, in consequence of lameness, were allowed to travel at leisure, upon condition of reaching Ghent by seven on the following morning; but that, having been prevented by the bad weather from arriving in time to procure billets, we would pay for lodging and supper; to this he readily agreed.

One of the drunken fellows in the room, rousing from his lethargy, wildly stared, and abruptly complimented us with the novel information that we were deserters; when the landlord, observing our apparent indignation, which he mistook for real, interposed in order to keep peace, and begged us to take no notice of it, as they were drunk; to which we feigned an unwilling acquiescence, but were, nevertheless, somewhat disconcerted;

however, he fell asleep again, and, soon after, they departed, too drunk to make any further observation.

Notwithstanding our fears and the garlic, we ate a most hearty supper; at midnight, after preparing everything for a start, in case of emergency, and all our clothes dry, we lay down on two beds, each keeping watch in turn, until four a.m. when we bought two flasks of spirits and some provisions.

The weather was fine, and not a creature stirring, but the landlord; we paid him, and departed. Without thinking of the road to Ghent, we turned to the left, when he called to us, "You are going wrong;" we thanked him, and proceeded as he directed. The door, however, was no sooner closed, than we crossed the street, one by one, crept silently past his house, and took the road to Bruges; so that, had there been any suspicion, this accidental occurrence must have thrown the chase off the scent.

Continuing our journey to the N. W., until dawn of Sunday, we entered a thick low wood, and here lay without disturbance, basking in the vivifying rays of the sun, and listening to the church bells summoning all good people to assemble. We would willingly have joined them, had the church been so secure an asylum as the wood. As Whitehurst, with a praiseworthy and religious sense of the dangers he was about to encounter, had packed his prayer-book in his knapsack, and preserved it through all his disasters, we read prayers, and offered up our humble thanksgivings for deliverance from the hand of the enemy.

About sun-set, it began to rain again, we quitted the wood, and proceeded to the westward, by a very bad road, frequently halting to rest, our feet being excessively tender. At about one a. m., we passed through a village, and took shelter, for some little time, from a very heavy shower, under a portico, and then went on through another village. At three, we crossed the high road to Bruges; a solitary public house was near, in which no one could be seen but an old woman, sitting by the fire; and being again thoroughly wet, we entered and asked for gin.

Many minutes had not elapsed before a Frenchman came in,

baited his horse, and departed, without addressing, or seeming to take the least notice of us. After regaling ourselves with eggs, and drying our clothes a little, we continued our march in the rain till near seven; then struck into a wood by the road side, and fortified ourselves with leaves as before. The rain fell in torrents, during the whole day, attended with repeated showers of hail. The increasing violence of the wind also, rendered the weather intensely cold, and caused such a perpetual chattering of the teeth, that it was difficult to articulate with sufficient distinctness to be understood. In addition to these sufferings, our feet were severely blistered. I had a tumour forming on my left side, which obliged me to lie always on the right, and proved the foundation of a rheumatism, which I much fear I shall feel through life.

Towards evening, the incessant fall of rain had so nearly inundated the wood, that, had we continued two hours longer, we must have been floated out of our nest Soon after five p. m. we proceeded by the main road; but it being very dark, we could no longer direct our course by the stars. About eight, we met a Fleming, of whom we inquired the road to Bruges, but through his misunderstanding us, we were induced to walk back a considerable distance. On passing a lone hut, we again asked the question, and were told not to quit the high road to the left; by this retrograde movement, we had marched about four miles unnecessarily; nevertheless, towards midnight we arrived at the gates of Bruges.

At this time, we were all in a most deplorable condition—wet to the skin, our feet bleeding, and so swollen, that we could scarcely walk at the rate of three miles an hour. Near the gates we observed a public house, and, having hitherto found such places to afford relief and safety, at this hour of the night, we entered, and saw nobody but an old woman and a servant; at first they appeared somewhat surprised, but asked no questions except such as regarded our wants, frequently exclaiming, "*pauvres conscripts.*"

We dried our clothes, when the sudden transition from cold to heat split Hunter's feet; several of his nails also were loose, and

Whitehurst had actually walked off two. The fire made us all so very sensitive, that we could scarcely bear a foot to the floor; but found some relief by bathing them in oil; having, however, enjoyed a comfortable supper, we laid ourselves down as before, keeping watch in turn, until four a. m., when we paid the old woman, and departed.

After wandering about in the dark, endeavouring to find out a road round the town, until break of day, we sought refuge in a neighbouring wood: here we reposed until three in the afternoon, screened by dead leaves: about that time a boy alarmed us. No sooner had he disappeared than we retreated, one by one, to a place of greater security, near a windmill, which, for the sake of distinction, was termed Windmill Wood. This was the second fine day since leaving Valenciennes, and the sun, diffusing its benign influence throughout our whole frame, so renovated our strength, that, forgetting our wounds, we felt equal to the severest trials.

At sun-set, the fort was again broken up, and, having had time during the day to consult the map, we marched directly to the bridge over the canal, doubled the town to the westward, and gained the road to the coast. About ten, being exceedingly fatigued from the difficulty of walking in the lacerated state of our feet, we thought of halting for the night; judging this to be more prudent, than going into increased danger with the certainty of being unequal to any sudden effort, or rapid retreat; however, unwilling to lose an hour, and dreading the probability of becoming weaker and worse, we determined to proceed.

About eleven, having gained only a mile in three quarters of an hour, we were compelled to halt, and bivouacked in an adjoining copse, exposed to severe cold and repeated showers.

At eight a. m., being surprised by an old woman collecting wood, who immediately fled in the utmost consternation, we decamped, deeming it imprudent to remain in any spot where we had been seen; scarcely had we quitted the copse, when two sportsmen were observed to enter it; we immediately jumped over a ditch, hobbled about two miles to the eastward, crept into an almost impenetrable thicket, and there remained in the rain till nine p m. We then gained the high road, and continued our route to Blankenberg, a village on the coast, a few miles to the eastward of Ostend.

At ten, passing by a solitary public house, we observed through the window, an old man, two women, and a boy, sitting round a comfortable fire, at supper. Hunter and I entered for the purpose of purchasing provisions to take on board any vessel we might be enabled to seize, being then about four miles from the sea. We asked for gin— the woman of the house rose and stared at us, apparently alarmed at our appearance; we repeated the demand without obtaining a reply; still gazing, for a few seconds, regardless of our request, she rapturously exclaimed, "*Mon Dieu, ce sont des Anglois,*" and immediately offered us chairs.

Somewhat disconcerted at this unexpected reception, we again asked for gin, to which she replied, "Take seats, and you shall have whatever my house can afford." We thanked her for the attention, and reiterated our request. She insisted we should partake of her fare, and assured us that not a soul should enter the house during our stay, if we would but sit down; we again refused, and observed, that, being conscripts, ordered into garrison at Blankenberg, we were fearful of punishment should we not arrive there that night.

She burst into a loud laugh, and ran to bar the door and window shutters, at the same time directing the servant to fry more ham and eggs; we assured her it was useless, as we had already taken supper at Bruges, and that we durst not stay, adding, it was a pretty compliment to us Frenchmen to call us English; she jocosely replied, "Well, then, you are not English, but it is so long since I saw any of my good folks, that I insist on your eating some ham and eggs with me; besides, you will not be able to get away from Blankenberg tonight."

We used every means in our power to dispossess her of her suspicions, to all which she only replied, "Take chairs, if it is only for a few minutes, and then *par complaisance* I will believe you." Her persevering deportment, bearing the almost certain stamp of sincerity, together with our hungry inclinations, induced us to accept the invitation, and partake of her luxuries, knowing there could be little danger, as Whitehurst and Mansell were on the lookout.

During our most comfortable regale, she talked of nothing but her dear English (notwithstanding our repeated endeavour to change the subject), and dwelt particularly on the happiness of her former life, when in the service of an English family. She uttered several broken sentences in English, of which we took not the slightest notice, but which confirmed in our minds the idea of her having lived some time where the language was spoken.

Being just about to rise, furnished with provisions for our companions, a loud rap announced someone at the door:—the woman started up, seized me by the arm, and, pushing me into the next room, exclaimed, "*Pour l'amour de Dieu par ici, les gens d'armes.*" Although we felt sure if was Whitehurst, yet we had no objection to see the result of this manoeuvre, and therefore made no resistance to her wishes, but complied with seeming reluctance. Still, as it was possible he might have knocked to warn us of the approach of someone, we followed her to the back door; at parting, she took me by the hand, and repeated her assurance of the impossibility of getting off from Blankenberg that night, and desired us to return, adding, "Good night, friends, I shall see you again."

Nothing but a thorough conviction of our being absconding prisoners of war, added to a sincere regard for the English, could have produced such conduct; certainly neither our actions nor accent betrayed us, for they were less foreign to the French than her own. No sooner had we regained the road, than our companions joined us; from them we learnt, that being alarmed at seeing the window closed, they were on the point of bursting open the door; when, peeping through the shutter, they saw everything that passed within, and, wishing to be of the party, gave the rap which alarmed our friendly hostess.

Continuing our march for the coast, we passed through a village about midnight, stopped occasionally to listen, with delight, to the pleasing monotony of the waves rolling over the beach, which, as we approached, created feelings of enjoyment that I had never before experienced. Between twelve and one a. m. we entered the village of Blankenberg, protected from the sea by the sand-bank. Observing a large gateway, apparently the road to the beach, I passed through to reconnoitre, leaving my companions in the street; to my great consternation, I found myself near a guard-house, and close to a sentry-box, from which I had the good fortune to retreat, unobserved.

Proceeding through the village, to the westward, and finding a footpath leading over the sand-bank, we ran down to the sea, forgetting our wounds, and exulting as though the summit of our wishes were attained, and we were on the point of embarkation. Indeed, so exquisite was the delight, that, regardless of consequences, we dashed into the water, drank of it, and splashed about like playful schoolboys, without being in the least disconcerted that the few vessels which could be seen were high and dry, close under the battery.

Nor will these feelings create surprise, when it is recollected, that more than five years had elapsed since we last quitted the sea in the Mediterranean, and that to regain it was considered as surmounting the principal obstacle to final success. But when these first transports had a little subsided, and were succeeded by rational reflection, we could but acutely feel the disappointment; although, had we been enabled properly to calculate the tides, we might have foreseen this event; for it was high water, on that day, about half-past five p. m., consequently low water about midnight, and, as the vessels cannot be launched from that flat beach, excepting about the last quarter of the flood, and the first of the ebb tides, we could not have gotten afloat, had we arrived even four hours earlier. [15]

---

15. A few days previously to my leaving England for the Mediterranean, in September, 1802, I asked my father how I was to get home, to pass my examination for lieutenant, when my six years as mid were completed. He replied, "Walk home across the continent." Thus, with the exception of a few miles, were his orders that night accomplished.

Our spirits, however, were not to be damped, and, notwithstanding our original intention was to make for Cadsand, we resolved to wait in the neighbourhood the issue of another night; to this end we returned by the same path, to the village, and, while going leisurely along the strand-street, heard a distant sound of the clashing of muskets, and footsteps of a body of men running; this was decidedly the guard, who had probably seen us from the heights.

We instantly doubled back, crossed by a bye-lane, leaped a ditch, and ran over the fields, until we judged ourselves out of reach of the pursuers. This was another instance of our narrowly escaping danger, which some may attribute to blind chance, but which, by us, was felt to be an interposition of Divine Providence in our favour; for there can be no doubt, that, had we continued two minutes longer on the beach, or had not the muskets' clash given the alarm, we certainly should have come in contact with the guard; the result of which would have been imprisonment, or, not improbably, death.

On regaining the high road, we consulted what measures to adopt; after some consideration, it was determined to revisit the "cabaret." We accordingly returned to an adjoining wood, and there lay until day dawned, when Hunter and myself proceeded to the house, and were told the old lady had not yet risen. The nature of our embassy not admitting of much time being wasted in "punctilious etiquette" we went to her chamber-door, and solicited an audience; this was readily granted, without any confusion, or even quitting her bed.

After the usual salutations, we apologized for our early call, attributing it to the commandant at Blankenberg having ordered us back to Bruges by seven o'clock; adding, that gratitude for her kindness, the preceding evening, had induced us to call *en passant*.

"Bah," she exclaimed, with a significant grin, "I told you, you could not get off from Blankenberg, and that I should see you again; sit down, we will have coffee, and then talk over matters;" at the same time ordering her son, a lad of about twelve years of age, to look out of the door and let her know when he saw any one coming; she then rose and dressed herself.

We were recommencing a train of compliments, for the purpose of bringing about the truth, when she exclaimed, "Hold your tongues, I knew that you were English gentlemen the moment I saw you." The whole tenor of her familiar and pithy style of address, convinced us of her sincerity, and we immediately offered one hundred pounds, to be divided between her and any boatmen who would undertake to land us and our comrades in England, or put us on board an English vessel.

"Comrades," she exclaimed, "what comrades?"

We replied, there were two others in the neighbouring wood, anxiously waiting our return, "Call them instantly," she said, "and twenty others if they are there; in three or four days you shall all be in England, or I am not an honest woman."

The signal was given; Whitehurst and Mansell promptly joined,——when, attempting to congratulate each other upon this auspicious occasion, we were so overpowered, so choked with joy that we could scarcely articulate; the tear of gratitude trickled down the cheek, whilst the hand of friendship simultaneously met that of its neighbour; even the old woman (notwithstanding her vivacity) could not refrain from participating in our feelings.

After cutting the money, amounting to about twenty pounds, out of our collars, to let our hostess see we were not penniless, we sat down to breakfast before a comfortable fire. She afterwards conducted us into a hay-loft, over a back room which was never made use of in winter, so that we were now in comparative safety; dependant, indeed, on the sincerity of the family. It was not, however, probable, they would prove treacherous; for, exclusively of the woman's apparent devotion to the English, the sum we proffered so much exceeded that of the French government, *viz.* 2*l* 1s 8d per head (for she, as well as ourselves, at the time, was ignorant of the reward offered at Valenciennes), that it would amply compensate for the risk.

The roof which now sheltered us, covered a solitary "caba-

View of the Raie-de-chat Showing Entrance to Loft

ret," situated midway between Bruges and Blankenberg, known by the sign of the "*Raie-de-chat*," which, by way of abbreviation, we called the "Cat," and being the house of police correspondence, it was visited regularly three times a week, and sometimes oftener, by the *gendarmes*, consequently the less likely to be suspected.

According to the "code Napoleon," the penalties attached to favouring the escape of prisoners of war, were a fine of 12*l* 10*s*, the expenses of the law proceedings, and two months' imprisonment. This law, however, did not intimidate Madam Derikre, for such was her name; she resolved upon serving us; yet, notwithstanding her apparent sincerity and assurance of success, our minds were not perfectly at ease until twenty-four hours had elapsed; that being the time allowed for proprietors to announce to the police the presence of strangers in their houses.

In order to excite confidence, we offered her all our money; this she generously refused, declaring that if success did not attend our exertions, she should not expect a *stiver*. No sooner were we in the loft, than, aided by our friendly hostess, our separate wounds were examined and dressed. After dark, the servant maid, named Cocher, and the dog Fox, being placed at the front door to watch, we descended to partake of some broth; anxiously waiting the return of a messenger sent by Madam Derikre to Blankenberg, for her confidential friend, a man named Winderkins. About nine, the boy came with intelligence, that he was gone to Ostend, and that his wife would send him to the "Cat" upon his return. We remounted into the loft, and slept as comfortably upon clean straw, as the pain of our wounds would allow.

The following evening, Mynheer Winderkins was introduced. He undertook, upon condition of sharing the reward, to find a fisherman who would either land us in England, or put us on board an English man of war, and promised information on the subject the following day. In continual expectation of the happy hour of departure, we remained in our snug retreat; receiving frequent messages from Winderkins until the 1st of December, when he appeared, and attributed his delay to the precautions necessary to be taken on so critical an occasion; but having at length succeeded, we were to hold ourselves in readiness to depart that night.

Soon after eight p. m., furnished with a few provisions, we quitted the "Cat," leaving with Madam Derikre bills to the amount of 50*l*, reserving the other fifty for Winderkins and the boatmen. In an hour we reached Blankenberg; followed our guide down the beach to the eastward of the village, and concealed ourselves amongst the sand-hills, whilst he went to apprise the fisherman of our arrival.

In this position we remained about two hours, Winderkins occasionally returning and desiring us to be particularly silent, there being several men on the beach, and the patrol on the alert. After a further absence of half an hour, he again returned, told us, we must be patient, and postpone the event to the next night, the tide having then ebbed so as to leave the vessels high and dry. We returned to the "Cat," much to the surprise of Madam Derikre.

The following day, Winderkins not appearing, the boy was despatched to learn the cause. About noon he returned with answer, that as there was not the slightest chance of success that night, he thought it imprudent to expose us to useless danger. We now began to suspect his fidelity, and thinking he might doubt the performance of our promise, it was agreed to give him half the remaining cash, and a bill of 30*l*, when on the beach, on condition that he fulfilled his engagement, or returned it

On the 3rd he appeared, and informed us, that in consequence of the fishermen having been unsuccessful, they had obtained permission to remain afloat a mile from the shore, and, provided no English vessel was seen, it was probable that that permission would be extended to several days; we must, therefore, be patient, and he would, upon the honour of a Fleming, insure success.

On the 4th he sent his daughter to say that all was well, and he would be with us in the evening. He kept his word: to insure his fidelity, we divided our money as before agreed, between him and Madam Derikre, having previously paid her the greater part of our twenty *louis* for food.

We now bade *adieu* to the "Cat," and, accompanied by Madam Derikre and Winderkins, proceeded to Blankenberg. After leaving us some time behind the sand-hills, the latter returned with information that he could not find the fisherman who had undertaken to embark us. It was instantly determined to seize one of the *schuyts*; we accordingly ran down to the beach, preceded by Winderkins as a lookout, gave him his bill, and leaped on board the outermost vessel; the sails were arranged and everything speedily prepared for weighing.

The night was dark, the wind fresh and favourable, the sea smooth and inviting; we sat silent as the grave, waiting with intense anxiety, until the tide, which was then flowing, should float our little bark. Whilst thus listening to the murmuring break of the sea, which seemed slowly to approach, as if chiding our impatience, yet inviting us to the protection of its bosom, our dearest hopes appeared upon the point of being realized.

These hopes, however, were but of short duration, and only tended to render our disappointment more bitter: the tide rose, just to cast a few sprays against the bows, and to retire. So high had our expectations been raised, that the water had receded some feet, ere we could believe it had left us; it was, then, however, too evident to be doubted. In so critical a situation, within pistol-shot of the fort, there was little time for deliberation; disappointed, but not disheartened, every article was replaced as it had been found, and we reluctantly withdrew, fully convinced, however, of the practicability of getting afloat from Blankenberg, if we did but seize the proper opportunity. It was, therefore, determined to repeat the attempt the following night, and, in the mean time, to re-occupy our old quarters.

In the morning, Winderkins sent to say, he had reason to suspect the fisherman had proved treacherous; that we had better not quit the "Cat," being there in perfect security; and that a day or two of patience might save us years of misery. The soundness of this reasoning made us content in the loft, until the evening of the 9th, when he came, and exultingly congratulated us upon the present certainty of success. "In two days," said Mynheer, "you shall be with your families, for I have now found a fisherman who will undertake the job, provided his vessel be restored to him." Of this we gave him every assurance, and he left us. After so irksome a state of suspense, we were the more elated at the now flattering prospect of a speedy restoration to our native shore.

On the 10th he returned, damping our hopes with information, that, in consequence of the appearance of several English vessels of war, all the fishing smacks were hauled above high water mark. Suspecting such repeated excuses originated either in fear, or incapacity to fulfil his engagement, it was determined to go again that night, so as to be on the beach at half flood. We, accordingly, departed towards midnight, and rendezvoused at his house; his daughters keeping watch at the doors, for it appeared all the family were in the secret.

Leaving my friends there, I went with Winderkins to the beach, and found the vessels as he had represented, except one, which was moored with five hawsers, about pistol-shot from the fort, just to the eastward of a *jetée*. I got on board to examine her sails, and to see that everything necessary could be got ready in an instant.

I found that the wind, being nearly on shore, we should be obliged to make aboard to the eastward, which, in a flat-bottomed craft, without sufficient ballast, the ropes and sails all covered with frozen snow, and a good deal of swell upon the beach, would have been of very doubtful issue: should, however, the wind shift only two points, there was a chance of success.

With this information I returned to my comrades, and we all went down to the beach, there watching the rise and fall of the tide; when, the impracticability of getting the vessel to sea, as the wind then stood, being evident, and seeing her again hard and fast, we returned to the country from the fourth trip. The next day, bad weather prevented the fishermen from going to sea, and obliged them to haul the vessels beyond the reach of the surf.

The hopes of getting away from Blankenberg being somewhat lessened, our attention was directed to other quarters. Winderkins was despatched to Ostend and Nieuport, to find what chance there was of succeeding in that neighbourhood, with instructions to return in forty-eight hours.

Three days, however, elapsed, without our hearing a word, and the continuance of bad weather rendered night excursions to Blankenberg useless. Repeated messengers were now sent, but no tidings of Mynheer. I therefore resolved upon going myself in disguise, for the double purpose of seeing if he were there, and of ascertaining the position of the *schuyts*. Equipped with Monsieur Derikre's great coat, large broad-brimmed hat, and canvas gaiters, and with scraps of paper directed to two of the inhabitants, under pretence of purchasing pigs, I set out at two in the afternoon, attended by old Cocher, the servant maid, who walked about fifty paces in advance.

On my arrival, Madam Winderkins received me in the utmost confusion. I questioned her upon her husband's delay; she told me she was apprehensive some accident had befallen him, or he certainly would not have failed in his promise. In the midst of our conversation, he entered, having visited the coast as far as Calais, without discovering any prospect of success more promising than at Blankenberg. He assured me, that not a craft, nor a boat of any kind, was to be seen in a situation whence it could be carried off.

After a fulsome train of compliments, upon the patience and perseverance we had hitherto displayed, he repeated his entire devotion to the cause, be the risk never so great, and promised, that during the detention of the fishing vessels, he would range the coast, and endeavour to find out other means of embarking.

I then went with him to the beach, and examined the precise situation of the *schuyts*. During an hour's promenade in this delightful, though perplexing, situation, an English brig hove in sight. I fear I might incur the imputation of bordering on the romantic, were I to attempt to describe the varied and conflicting sensations by which I was agitated at again beholding the British flag; nor can I say, what risks I would not have hazarded in order to get afloat, had there been a boat at hand; in which case, I, of course, should have returned in the night, to carry off my comrades. I left this scene with reluctance, and returned to the "Cat," previously directing Winderkins to go the following day towards Flushing.

On the 16th, he returned without any satisfactory information; but he was enabled to assure us, that it was utterly impossible to seize the Flushing packet-boat, as we had intended, every passenger being strictly examined, and his passport proved, before he was suffered to embark; so that our hopes seemed limited to Blankenberg. He also assured us, that the number and vigilance of the patrol were such, that an attempt to range the coast would be attended with certain capture.

This intelligence, anything but cheering, made it difficult to decide upon the best mode of proceeding; but, being still persuaded of the possibility of getting afloat from Blankenberg, it was determined to make another effort before we left that part of the coast. Madam Derikre informed us, that the cause of Winderkins' delay, when despatched to the westward, was—his going to Dunkirk, where he had a private conference with a banker, who expressed a favourable opinion of the bill we had given him, as he had before negotiated others with the same signature; but he advised Winderkins not. to make use of it at present—observing, at the same time, that he was aware the gentleman had eloped. This information, no doubt, urged him to persevere in our behalf, and was also an additional stimulant to the avowed friendship of the Derikres.

In the evening, Winderkins sent word that the vessels were all preparing for sea; but the next morning our expectations were again disappointed, by information that the government had laid an embargo on all the Blankenberg craft, until they furnished five seamen for the navy. The vessels were again hauled up above high water mark, and the fishermen fled in all directions.

We now thought of making our way into Holland; but the severity of the weather, the extreme difficulty of penetrating into that country, the want of means to travel, combined with the dissuasion of Madam Derikre and Winderkins, who repeated their assurances of shelter and assistance, induced us to remain in our present situation.

In the daily hope of a favourable change, we continued in the loft, but were occasionally in some danger; for the house was seldom without *gendarmes*, custom-house officers, or foot soldiers, looking out for the seamen, The door of our loft was, however, kept shut, and the ladder, by which only it was accessible, placed over head, in the stable, out of sight. Day after day elapsed, without any relaxation in this decree.

Feeling how precarious was our situation, Hunter and I proposed to reconnoitre the woods, in order to find out the most secure asylum, in the event of being disturbed. About two p.m., the boy first looking out to see if the coast was clear, we sallied forth on the high road to Bruges, but had scarcely gone a mile, when two horse *gendarmes* were observed coming towards us: being then near a gate, we struck off into a large ploughed field, surrounded with wood, and, when screened from the *gendarmes* by the hedge, took to our heels.

It appeared, that, no sooner did they observe us turn off the road, than they galloped for the gate; for they entered the field just as we were about to reach the wood. Luckily, there was a wide ditch, so overflowed, that part of the wood was inundated; we instantly plunged in, swam over, escaped into the interior, and there lay concealed until dark, when we rejoined our friends in the loft.

To our surprise we learnt from Madam Derikre, that she had heard of our adventure from the *gendarmes*, who, halting to bait, told her, they were very nearly catching two of the Blankenberg sailors, "but the rogues swam like ducks." This narrow escape was a warning to be more cautious. I mention it, because it was the only act we committed, which had not an object in view worth the risk. We, consequently, now confined ourselves to the

Pursued by *Gendarmes*

loft, receiving from, and sending messages to, Winderkins.

At this time, we occasionally amused ourselves by writing, in French, bulletins of our proceedings from the 16th of November; and it is upon these memoranda that this *Narrative* is principally grounded. On the 2nd of January, information was brought that two of the vessels had been nearly floated by the last tide.

Upon the receipt of this joyful news, it was resolved to pay them a visit that night; the wind being from the eastward, and the weather fine, our hopes were most sanguine, amounting almost to a confidence of immediate departure. Accordingly, soon after eleven, we went down to the coast, and remained behind the sand-hills as before, until the tide rose within a few feet of one of the vessels, which was found embedded in the ice and snow; we, however, jumped on board, and, in this situation, remained about twenty minutes, in the anxious hope that every succeeding wave would lift her bows; but, the tide ebbing, we were obliged to retire.

The next night, we again proceeded to "Mynheer's" house, who seemed to consider it the last time they should see us; "Tomorrow," he observed, "we shall all be *chez nous*." When the tide had risen within a few feet of its utmost height, Hunter and I got on board the same vessel as before, and made several preparations, that there might be no delay or confusion, when she floated. So soon as all was ready, we ran to the other two, with the joyful information. On our way thither, Hunter expressed some doubt, which proved nothing but an untimely difference of opinion. The exact state of the vessel I represented to Whitehurst and Mansell, who, always ready to run any risk, rather than suffer the slightest chance of success to escape, coincided with me in the propriety of making the attempt. Hunter, believing it useless, declined attending.

Nevertheless, we three instantly repaired on board, let slip the stern-fasts, and began to heave upon the bow hawser. Each wave, as it rolled in, lifted the vessel, and, having hove a taut strain, she crept seaward about a foot every rise, falling upon the sand, with a shock almost sufficient to drive the mast through her bottom.

We exerted every nerve, and had got her out about ten fathoms, when, to our mortification the tide receded faster than we could heave ahead; soon after, she became immoveable.

On jumping ashore, Hunter rejoined us, and, in justice I should add, was exceedingly distressed at his previous decision, as the result proved that his additional strength would have enabled us to get to sea. We were thus obliged to return to the "Cat."

In the morning, Winderkins entreated us to remain quiet, as various rumours, relative to the moving of the vessel were in circulation; some attributed it to the unusual height of the tides, whilst others confidently asserted that an attempt had been made to steal her. This dispute was productive of no other evil, than an order to haul the vessels higher up; that, however, was sufficient to deprive us of all hope of getting away from Blankenberg until the embargo was taken off; we, therefore, consulted upon other means, when Madam Derikre agreed to go to Bruges, and advise with a friend of hers, named Moitier, with whom she had before been leagued, in unlawful practices respecting conscripts. To guard against treachery on his part, she was instructed in the following tale:—

> A young Englishman, late a prisoner of war, is concealed at Flushing, and offers 50*l* to anyone who will land him in England, or cause him to be put on board an English vessel.

In the event of succeeding, my plan was to get away, and return in the night to carry off my comrades; but they, unwilling that I should leave them, proposed that Mansell should be the one to effect this, believing, that with his smooth face, he might pass, in disguise, for a girl. Moitier, at first delighted at this new source of acquiring wealth, readily assented, but was afterwards intimidated by the apprehension of this Englishman being a spy of the French government, and, as he was at that time under its particular "surveillance," for other illegal deeds, declined interfering.

A few days elapsed without hearing anything further upon the subject, when Madam Derikre was again despatched to him; she returned with the information that he would be at the "Cat" in a day or two. In the mean time, Winderkins was reconnoitring east and west, ignorant of her having consulted Moitier. In fact, all parties were equally desirous of forwarding our views, and, therefore, the more anxious to prevent our quitting this part of Flanders.

On the 11th, we wrote a letter to the commander-in-chief, off Flushing, and gave it to Winderkins, who was desired to offer a bribe to anyone who would put it on board an English ship; but we had no reason to believe it reached its destination.

On the 12th, we again sent Madam Derikre to Moitier, who now consented to go immediately to Flushing, and make an agreement with a smuggler, promising information on the subject in a very few days. Our hopes being thus kept continually alive by new projects, without any definitive arrangement, it was again debated whether we should remain in the loft or march into Holland: the former was determined on until the result of Moitier's trip to Flushing should be known; our present comparative security being preferable to a dangerous uncertainty, particularly as we were convinced that it was the interest, as well as the most anxious desire of all our friends, to effect our departure.

On the 14th, we were overjoyed to learn, from Winderkins, that the embargo was taken off, and the vessels all preparing for sea. This joy, however, was not of long duration; for, on going to Blankenberg the next evening, we found that not a vessel had been launched, and that the permission to go to sea, was but a *ruse de guerre*, to entrap the seamen required for the navy. Winderkins, alarmed at our presence, requested us immediately to retreat to the country, for the whole of the police were, oat, lying in ambush for the sailors. In order to insure our safety, and to give the signal to disperse, if necessary, he marched on before, through bye-paths, until we regained the "Cat."

On the 16th he sent word, that, the five seamen having been

taken, the extra police was withdrawn. The night being very dark, we ventured down, and found that some of the vessels had been to sea, but were replaced in their former positions. The following night, knowing the tide would rise gradually higher, the jaunt was repeated. But the recent circumstance of one having dragged her anchors, as was supposed, induced them to obey the commandant's order. At this time we learnt, that Moitier was gone from Flushing to Holland, determined to find a smuggler who would assist this young Englishman, for he was still ignorant of our number.

On the 25th, Winderkins, having been daily pressed for the fulfilment of his engagement, to find a fisherman to take us off, but which he had as often evaded under one frivolous pretext or other, was obliged to confess that all his endeavours had been hitherto unavailing, and that he at length despaired of success.

It was now evident that we must depend upon our own exertions alone, to gain possession of a vessel, if we persevered in the attempt to embark at Blankenberg. He, however, undertook to continue on the lookout, whilst we seized a boat: this, indeed, was a very important service; he was a sergeant of the national guard, and frequently on duty at Blankenberg; consequently, not only the less likely to be suspected, but able occasionally to give a turn to the conversation at the fort, which might otherwise excite increased vigilance.

We, therefore, gave him for past services, and as a retaining fee, a bill of 15l, instead of the 30l, which, with what he had already received, amounted to about 17l. He expressed his gratitude and vowed to deserve it. A few days elapsed in this state of uncertainty, during which, we occasionally received messages from both Bruges and Blankenberg, serving to keep us in continual expectation of the morrow bringing forth something decisive.

On the 2nd of February, having again journeyed to Blankenberg, we found the tide to approach within a very few feet of two of the vessels. The following night, the excursion was repeated, when the same vessels were lying with their bows awash, but there was not sufficient water to float them. We were now completely puzzled how to act: could cash have been raised, we had resolved upon marching into Holland, for the thoughts of continuing any longer in a state of inactivity became insupportable. Money, however, could not be procured: we were, therefore, compelled to remain in the loft.

Scarcely a day passed without something occurring to revive our hopes until the 17th, when Winderkins again appeared, and told us the evening tide would float one of the vessels; we, therefore, at a proper hour, went to his house, and thence to the beach, most anxiously watching the roll of every wave; but, as if fortune had doomed us to be the shuttlecock of her caprice, our hopes appeared excited only to put to proof our patience and perseverance; the water receded, without reaching a single vessel. Very bad weather setting in, attended with heavy falls of snow and hail, rendered night excursions to any distance almost impracticable.

Madam Derikre proposed our being below at night, for the covering of the loft being nothing but open tiling, through which the wind blew from three sides, we were frequently benumbed with cold, particularly as we durst not move about to take exercise. This offer was readily accepted, one keeping watch at the door all night, regularly relieved, and occasionally assisted by our friend Fox. Being now more comfortably lodged, we forsook the loft entirely; occupying in the day a place about eight feet by four, with a door opening directly upon the wood. Many schemes were suggested, but none sufficiently tempting to induce us to shift our quarters, during the present inclement weather.

One project was that I should go in disguise to Moitier: and I consulted Madam Derikre, who insisted on apprising him of my intention, that he might not be absent. Moitier, however, declared he would have nothing to do with the affair if I attempted to approach his house; promising, at the same time, to give me a conference at the "Cat," in the course of the week. The week, however, expired without our seeing him; but a message was brought to the effect that he had again been to Flushing, and that we should see him ere long.

Among the various schemes that were suggested in our repeated and fruitless jaunts to Blankenberg, it was proposed to procure shovels, and in the first dark and rainy night to dig a channel in the sand up to one of the schuyts, so as to admit of the tide flowing high enough to float her. Madam Derikre had agreed to furnish these tools and to look out, whilst her son and Winderkins assisted in the operation; but not being able to procure shovels, the experiment was never tried, nor indeed would it have been mentioned, except to prove, that our minds were never idle in the furtherance of our object.

On the 1st of March, Winderkins came, and assured us, that everything had been so long quiet at Blankenberg, that the fishermen were gradually neglecting to haul the vessels up, and that he was certain the next spring tide would float several. Upon going the following night, we found them situated as he had described, though none were yet within reach of the water.

On the 3rd, we waited until the tide began to ebb; it, however, only broke against the bows of two or three: but as it had considerably gained, and would still increase the two next tides, we again encouraged a hope of the speedy termination of our troubles, and the final accomplishment of our object.

With heart elate, as in the moment of victory, on the night of the 4th of March, I made my thirteenth and last trip to Blankenberg, and, leaving my comrades at "Mynheer's" house, went with him to the beach to reconnoitre; when, finding several vessels nearly afloat, we returned to our party with the joyful information.

Furnished with provisions, and a lantern, we took a friendly leave of Winderkins' family, proceeded silently to the water's edge, and jumped on board the easternmost vessel, in the pleasing confidence of having at length evaded the vigilance of the enemy, and of being on the eve of restoration to our native soil. The wind was fresh and squally from the W. N. W., with a good deal of swell; the moon, although only three days after the full, was so obscured by dark clouds, that the night was very favourable for our purpose.

The vessel was moored by five hawsers; two ahead, and three astern: it was arranged, that Whitehurst and Mansell should throw over-board the latter, Hunter and I the former; this was preferred to cutting them. We had been so long in Flanders, and received such protection from the natives, that all harsh feeling which might have existed towards an enemy was so mellowed into compassion for their sufferings under the Corsican yoke, that we were unwilling to injure one of them, and therefore had determined, if in our power, to send back the craft, which being a fishing *schuyt*, might probably be the only support of an indigent family. Whilst Whitehurst and Mansell were executing the duty allotted to them, Hunter and I got ready the foresail, and paid [16] overboard one of the hawsers.

The tide now rolled in, the vessel floated, and we hove her out to within about four fathoms of her buoy. Whitehurst and I being ready to cut the other hawser, and hoist the sail, Hunter went to the helm, when he found the rudder was not shipped, but lying on the poop. We instantly ran aft, and got it over the stern, but the vessel pitched so heavily, that it was not possible to ship the lower pintle. We were now apprehensive of the total failure of the attempt; for, to go to sea without a rudder would have been madness, and being nearly under the battery, we were in momentary expectation of being fired into.

Several minutes were passed in this state of anxiety and danger, still persevering in the attempt to ship the rudder, but at length, finding it impossible, without a guide below, and feeling that our only hope was dependent upon the success of this important effort, in the excitement of the moment I jumped overboard: at the same instant, the vessel springing a little ahead, and the sea washing me astern, it was not without the greatest exertion I could swim up to get hold of the stern-post. Hunter, seeing that I was dashed from her by every wave, threw me a rope; this I made fast round my waist, and then, with some trouble, succeeded in shipping the rudder.

The effort of swimming and getting on board again, although

---

16. Let run fathom after fathom.

assisted by my comrades, so completely exhausted me, that I lay on my back for some time, incapable of moving a limb; but at length rallying, I went forward to help hoist the foresail, whilst Hunter cut the hawser, and then ran to the helm. The sail was no sooner up than the vessel sprang off, as if participating in our impatience, and glorying in our deliverance; such, however, is the uncertainty and vanity of all human projects, that at the very moment when we believed ourselves in the arms of liberty, and our feelings were worked up to the highest pitch of exultation, a violent shock suddenly arrested our progress.

We flew aft, and found that a few fathoms of the starboard quarter hawser having been accidentally left on board, as it ran out, a kink was formed near the end, which, getting jammed between the head of the rudder and the stern-post, had brought the vessel up all standing; the knife was instantly applied, but the hawser was so excessively taut and hard, that it was scarcely through one strand ere the increasing squall had swung her round off upon the beach.

At this critical juncture, as a forlorn hope, we jumped out to seize another vessel, which was still afloat; when Winderkins, seeing a body of men running upon the top of the sand hills, in order to surround us, gave the alarm: we immediately made a resolute rush directly across, leaving our knapsacks, and everything but the clothes on our backs, in the vessel; the summit was gained just in time to slip over on the other side unseen.

We ran along the hills towards the village for about a hundred yards, when, mistaking a broad ditch for a road, I fell in, but scrambled out on the opposite side. Mansell, who was close at my heels, thinking that I had jumped in on purpose, followed; this obliged the others to jump also. Thus was the pursuit of the enemy unexpectedly cut off, and a safe retreat to the "Cat" providentially secured.

We regained our headquarters in about three-quarters of an hour, and related this heart-rending disaster to Madam Derikre. Fearful that some of the many articles left in the vessel would give a clue to our late abode, and be the means of causing a strict search, she was desired to destroy everything that could lead to discovery, or suspicion; then taking all the bread in the house, and leaving Mansell there, the rest immediately set out for Windmill Wood, on the other side of Bruges, where we arrived a little before daylight.

It had been previously agreed, that Mansell should go in disguise, as a girl, to Moitier, and detail the whole truth, for he was still ignorant of there being four of us. Mansell was to procure a pair of shoes for each, some provisions, as much cash as he could raise, and, in his girl's dress, bring these articles out to us. Should he succeed in this, our intention was to quit Flanders, and walk through France and Germany, to Trieste, in the gulf of Venice; for, having previously learnt that the entire coast of Holland was guarded with as great strictness as that of Flanders, we had abandoned the idea of penetrating into that country.

Although, before this catastrophe, it had not been arranged that Mansell should be introduced to Moitier, for the purpose of getting away, and returning in the night to take off the others, yet, knowing from his youth, that he was incapable of undertaking the journey at present meditated, we were now unanimous that he should profit by this chance.

Not having had time to dry our clothes at the "Cat," we were in a most deplorable state, shivering with cold, and wet to the skin; the extremities of our garments solid boards of ice, and not a shoe amongst us worthy the name. In this wood we remained three days, each succeeding hour seeming to redouble the sufferings of the last; for, besides bodily exposure, the knowledge that we must fly the coast, and traverse the continent at this inclement season, without a certainty of adequate means, excited the keenest anxiety.

As Mansell did not appear with the promised supplies, we concluded he had either forgotten the situation, or was taken prisoner; and, being apprehensive that Moitier had proved treacherous, I reproached myself for having consented to expose him to this danger.

The stock of provisions was now almost expended, and, being incapable of marching any distance for want of shoes, it was resolved to return to the vicinity of the "Cat," in the hope of learning the fate of Mansell and of being there supplied with necessaries for our projected journey. We set out at eleven o'clock, and, reaching a neighbouring wood, about one a. m., halted to listen; being apprehensive that if any article had been found in the vessel to create suspicion of the "Cat," that *gendarmes* would be lying in ambush ready to butcher us. It was arranged, that Whitehurst and Hunter should remain under the hedge of the orchard, whilst I approached the house; and, in the event of my meeting with such numbers, as to render their assistance unavailing, I was to give the alarm, and they were to fly, regardless of me.

With firm, yet cautious step, I advanced, crept through a gap in the hedge, and entered the orchard, looking around, and listening like the timid deer, for the approach of the savage hound, whose thirst nothing but blood can satiate: starting, as by electricity, at a cold touch on my hand, I involuntarily threw myself into an attitude of defence, but seeing nothing, and judging that coward fancy had created this alarm, I again advanced, when I perceived by my side the dog Fox, whose cold mark of recognition in the dark, had been the cause of it, and who, trotting before me to the house, every now and then returned, as if to invite, and assure me that no enemy was near.

Having reached the window, I gently tapped; Madam Derikre opened it, begged me not to come in, and sent the dog to look out My first and most anxious inquiry was, of the doubtful fate of Mansell; she said, that she had escorted him to Moitier's disguised as a girl, had left him there, and had not seen him since. She then related that, soon after her return, the house was surrounded and minutely searched by thirty-six *gendarmes* and police officers, without their finding anything to corroborate their suspicions.

During our residence in the loft, we had procured five sticks, and put spike nails, with a sharp edge and point into the ends, to use as weapons of defence; four of these were taken in the vessel, the fifth we had given to young Derikre, who incautiously left it by the fireside; fortunately it was not noticed, or it would have been sufficient proof to implicate the whole family. She likewise related, that the lantern, having been known to belong to Winderkins, his house was also searched, and both of them were taken before the police. He confessed that the lantern was his property, but swore he had lent it to Madam Derikre; this she acknowledged, stating, that she had put it out of the door in lieu of her lamp, sent to be repaired, and that someone had stolen it.

The baker, who was also taken before the mayor, proved that the consumption of bread at the "Cat," had been more than doubled, for several weeks; this, however, was evaded by a declaration of an unusual increase of custom, to which she could safely swear, without risk or perjury. This explanation did not entirely clear her of suspicion; the house was again surrounded, and searched on the second night, but with no better success.

Being, therefore, in apprehension of surprise, she requested me not to come too near, and agreed to go to Moitier, in order to borrow some money for us, and procure shoes. I described to her the spot near which we intended to conceal ourselves; and then, provided with some bread, gin, and cold potatoes, returned to my comrades.

We now retreated to a thick wood, about three miles to the westward, and remained there without hearing from the Derikres until noon of the 10th, when a rustling amongst the bushes, set us all upon the *qui vive*. I crept forward, and, having listened attentively for a few moments, to my great joy perceived it was occasioned by our faithful friend, Fox, who having hunted us out in our new abode, now fawned upon us, apparently as much elated at the meeting as ourselves. On going with him in the direction whence he came, I found his young master bringing cheese and eggs.

We had been so long together, that this youngster became really attached to us, and, on the recital of our hardships and sufferings, he was so struck with the view of our camp, which was fortified with twigs made into basket work, that the kind-hearted boy burst into a flood of tears. We learnt from him, that his mother had been to Bruges, but that not finding Moitier at home, she was afraid to say a word to his wife. She had, however, seen Mansell, who was concealed in the house, he told her that he had not been able to procure money, and that he had gone out to Windmill Woody but' that his search for us had been ineffectual. This afterwards proved incorrect, for not being able to obtain supplies, he never made the attempt She also learnt that Moitier was gone into Holland, and was expected back in the course of the week. All this the boy related with as much feeling as if he thought our situation the most deplorable and wretched that human nature could endure. He promised to bring us bread and eggs, so long as we remained in the neighbourhood, but thought it much better to be in prison than to perish with cold in the woods.

In order to recompense him for his trouble, and to insure his future assistance, I made him a present of my watch, the only valuable I possessed.

Two days more were passed in this basket fort, when we were alarmed by the approach of an old peasant; well knowing that the Flemings entertained the utmost horror of the conscription, we passed ourselves off for conscripts. The old man seemed to sympathize in our distresses, and promised to bring us a loaf of bread; but, as it would have been imprudent to have suffered him to depart and to have waited his return, he was kept in conversation until nearly dark, and when he left us, we broke up the camp and fled.

Scarcely had we gone a mile, following each Other at some little distance, when Fox and his master were discovered: he advised us to go to a thick wood about two miles east of the house, and gave information of Moitier's return.

Soon after our taking up this position, the weather set in intensely cold, and, literally clad in armour of ice, we lay listening to the whistling wind, and shivering with exposure to the chilling blast, which not only defied repose, but threatened the most calamitous effects; indeed, the limbs were sometimes so benumbed, that it became absolutely indispensable to shake and twist ourselves about, to promote the necessary circulation of the blood.

Nor did there appear any prospect of the termination of this misery, but in death; for as the black and ponderous clouds passed swiftly over us, the wind increased, the hail beat furiously down, the trees trembled, and buckled to the squalls, until the raging violence of the storm seemed to threaten the uprooting of the very wood we occupied.

In this exposed situation, with variable, though piercing cold weather, we remained until the 15th, when the boy, with the help of Fox, again traced us out, and said, his mother had seen and detailed to Moitier our exact situation. He pretended surprise, declared that Mansell had never given him reason to suppose that he had companions, and, lamenting at the same time his inability to be of service at present, promised assistance in a day or two. This affectation of surprise, and assertion of Mansell's silence, we suspected to be an excuse only to detain us in the neighbourhood, by keeping alive our hopes of aid, until he saw what profit he was likely to make of Mansell; little caring what severe reflections he was thereby casting upon the lad's character. Whatever may have been the fact, we could obtain neither shoes nor supplies of any kind to enable us to depart, although kept in daily expectation of them.

Whitehurst now suffered so severely from illness, that doubts arose as to the possibility of his continuing much longer in this state of exposure, and had not his complaint taken a favourable turn, patience and fortitude must soon have yielded to the sinking energies of nature. In addition to our anxiety for the sufferings of our companion; a degree of gloomy restlessness pervaded every thought, auguring nothing but evil; but whether these feelings proceeded from pain and despondency, from experience of the past, or bore any affinity to that instinctive foresight which teaches the tenants of the forest to prepare for tempestuous weather, I will not determine.

With this presentiment, however, we prevailed on the boy

to bring a horse-cloth, and as neither of us had a second coat, it proved one of the greatest comforts I had ever experienced. Indeed, it so renovated our strength that we were more firmly bent than ever upon marching into Germany; but the increasing severity of the season confined our attention to present preservation, rather than heedlessly running into greater dangers. The dark and cheerless clouds, upon which our eyes were continually fixed, soon discharged flakes of snow in such profusion, as to threaten our being cut off from the "Cat;" but in order to prevent the too frequent passing and repassing, by which we might be retraced in the snow, Madam Derikre very considerately sent us a stock of bread, gin, and a little meat, which were economized to the best advantage.

At the commencement of the fall of snow, we moved about the wood, and finding a hollow, from which a tree had been dug, we laid a quantity of twigs in it, so as to make a dry bed; the horse cloth was then spread loosely over, propped up by a stick in the centre, fastened down with pegs, and. dead leaves strewed round the edge, thus forming a kind of tent; one corner was left open for the free admission of air, and for our own entrance and exit.

Here we lay in such comfort, that the sensation experienced can only be imagined by comparing it to turning into a warm bed after being nearly frozen to death. The snow falling all night, in the morning our nest was covered nearly a foot deep, and scarcely rose sufficiently above the surrounding white surface, to indicate the place of our concealment. It being almost impossible to travel in such weather, we determined patiently to wait its breaking up; unless, indeed, Moitier, in the meantime, should furnish us with sufficient supplies to justify a fresh movement.

Very little change occurred until the 19th, when we again despatched a messenger to Bruges, with a note to Mansell; but, as we received no answer, it was, doubtless, intercepted; it being Moitier's policy to prevent communication between us. A sudden thaw almost inundated the wood, and it was with much difficulty that the boy could get to our retreat with provisions.

In the Wood Coming Out From Under the Horse-Blanket

On the morning of the 21st, he came, almost out of breath, with information, that a party of men were again about to surround the house, and, it was supposed, to search the adjoining woods.

Upon this, we instantly broke up our camp, threw our bed of twigs in all directions, and ran through the woods a mile due east. A ditch, about eighteen feet wide, now presented itself before us; luckily, at a little distance, was a piece of timber lying across, upon which we passed without a moment's delay, and being too well versed in military tactics to leave the bridge for the enemy, it was drawn over, and thrown into a hedge.

Our hasty retreat was continued about three miles, when reaching an almost impenetrable thicket, we crept in and hid ourselves. In this thicket we lay some time, expecting every moment the approach of the pursuers; but, as we occupied a very favourable position for retreat, the surrounding woods being intersected with wide ditches, one of which was immediately in our rear, we were in no very great apprehension for the issue.

In the midst of our consultation, a distant noise was indistinctly heard, which seemed gradually to approach, until the actual motion of the bushes put an end to all doubt. We instantly jumped up, ready to fly, when a dog was discovered drawing near, and not far behind, some person penetrating through the thick wood; but, ere we had time to decide, our faithful friend Fox burst to view, fawning and curling himself in silent congratulation, as if sensible of a narrow escape: almost at the same moment came his affectionate master, who brought information, that a body of *gendarmes* only halted at his mother's, on their way to Blankenberg, but fancying they were come to make another search, he immediately ran off to give us timely notice.

The keen lad, guided by the sagacious Fox, had followed our footsteps, until he came to the broad ditch, when finding the bridge gone, and suspecting we had pulled it over, he had run round a considerable distance; having so done, he returned to the opposite bank, and continued hunting us up. We immediately retraced our steps, replaced the bridge, and marched back to our *trou*, which was rendered as comfortable as before. This little trip, we fancied, did us good, from the exercise it afforded.

A heavy fall of rain during two days, prevented the boy from getting to us; and, apprehensions were now entertained, that, from the overflowing of the ditches, and the almost inundated state of the woods, we should be compelled, by hunger, to expose ourselves in the day; although, in preference, we had resolved to endure the utmost extremity of privation. Indeed, we already felt the want of food; our fare was seldom more than bread, sometimes potatoes, and occasionally eggs, though a few days previously we had had a little meat, the bones of which were thrown away; but such was my state of hunger, that for these I now searched, and felt delight in finding one, which I ground down with a canine voracity, reproaching myself for my previous extravagance.

At length, hunger and wet forced us to quit the camp, and, about ten at night, approaching the "Cat," two of us went in, dried our clothes, and got something to eat, whilst the third, with Fox, kept watch at the door. The sagacity of this dog was really wonderful, Madam Derikre assured us, that latterly, this faithful animal, as if he knew our enemies, growled at every gendarme he saw, although he had been in the habit of seeing, and being caressed by them almost every day of his life. She again said, that Moitier had promised to assist us the moment Mansell was gone. Our hopes being somewhat enlivened by these repeated assurances, it was determined to wait a few days longer, could we survive the cold, to see the result of Mansell's departure.

We now ventured to pay nightly visits to the "Cat," in order to procure provisions, taking each time a different direction, to avoid making a path. One night, Whitehurst, exhausted with illness and fatigue, while crossing a ditch, fell in, and swinging, with his face upwards, under an old tree that overhung the water, it was with some difficulty we could extricate him. After this accident, we always left him in the nest; but Hunter and I continued our nightly excursions to the "Cat," and found its inmates at each succeeding visit, more and more determined to persevere in rendering us assistance; indeed, so much had we grown upon their esteem, and so intense was the interest excited by our extreme sufferings, that, on one occasion, poor old Cocher, the servant, offered to pawn even her gold cross and heart, and all she possessed, to Moitier, if he would but befriend the poor "Englishers."

About this time, Madam Derikre's visits to Moitier were so frequent, that he, at length, forbade them. She, however, learnt that Mansell had embarked for England, with a smuggler, in an open boat, fifteen feet in length. This was a great point, and our hopes were once more turned towards the coast, in the full expectation that he would return in the night, with a boat to take us off; or in some manner send us assistance, but day after day passed without intelligence.

Moitier not having fulfilled his promise of sending us supplies, so soon as Mansell was gone; and, indeed, seeming to have forbidden any further communication between us, by refusing to admit Madam Derikre; I determined—in spite of his previous threat, that he would have nothing to do with the affair if I attempted to approach his house—to go to Bruges, and see him myself; nor was this a hasty, though then an unconcerted resolution; for, notwithstanding we had been nearly a month in this dreary wilderness, exposed to the severest weather, and the keenest distresses, with clothes worn to threads;—notwithstanding my comrades had hitherto, evinced no impatience at the doubtful result of our protracted sufferings, which they would have seen multiplied to the utmost extremity of human endurance, rather than have been taken; and, notwithstanding my confidence, in their perseverance; yet so strong was their repugnance to separation, and my belief of their disapproval of the attempt, that I judged it more prudent to take this step, without consulting them, than to enter into a discussion which might create an unpleasant difference of opinion; and, as it could not involve them in danger, the odium, and consequent punishment attendant on failure, would fall solely on myself.

With this view of the measure, on the night of the 31st of

March, so soon as Hunter relieved me in watch, at the door, and we were ready to return to the woods, I communicated to him my plans; adding, that if they neither saw, nor heard from me the next day, they might rest assured, I had fallen into the hands of the enemy, and might then act for themselves, He in vain endeavoured to shake my determination, but, after the maturest deliberation, as I was convinced of the practicability of the project, and had taken my resolution, we shook hands, and parted.

After making the necessary arrangements with Madam Derikre, I lay down in the stable with my friend Fox at the door, who seemed to watch with increased vigilance, as if aware of the importance of his trust. My bed, in this solitary cell, was certainly not one of roses, for, independently of the anxiety arising from the fear of surprise, I at first felt something like compunction, at not having previously consulted my companions; nor was I without apprehension, that they might suspect I intended to desert them; and, should anything occur to cause the capture of either party during our separation, the report of such a disgraceful act might be circulated, without my ever being able to prove its fallacy: but the evident necessity for some decided step, and the conscious rectitude of my intention, presently dissipated such thoughts, and created a cheering presentiment that my plans would lead to a favourable result.

Satisfied, therefore, that I was acting for the best, I lay meditating a variety of schemes, as to the best mode of performing the task, till about four o'clock, scarcely able to close my eyes: at that hour, I gently tapped at Madam Derikre's window; she immediately equipped me in the same dress I had worn to Blankenberg on the 15th of December, and furnished me with a carpenter's rule, line, chalk, &c.

After taking some refreshment, we set out *tête-a-tête* for Bruges. At dawn of day, we separated, keeping about a hundred yards apart, and entered the town, just as the labourers were going to work. In passing the guard at the gates, I was chalking and rubbing out figures upon the rule, as if my mind was wholly occupied in my business. Although, I did not turn my head, I could, nevertheless, observe, from under my broad brim, two *gendarmes* eyeing me from head to foot; I, however, trudged on, uninterrupted, and followed the guide from street to street, until we entered that in which Moitier lived.

Fortunately not a creature was to be seen; on passing his door, she made a momentary pause, placing her hand on her hip, as a signal to me, and then went on, without looking behind her. I knocked, and asked for "*Monsieur*," but he was not at home. Upon inquiring for "*Madame*," she appeared; I told her that my business was of such importance, as absolutely to require my seeing "*Monsieur son epoux*;" and, if she would permit it, I wished to wait his return.

She politely shewed me into an apartment, but seeing it to be a public waiting-room, and being desirous of privacy, I made one or two observations remotely bearing upon the purport of my visit; when, finding she entertained no suspicion of who I was, I ventured to congratulate her upon the success her husband had met with respecting Mansell. "*Manselle*," she emphatically exclaimed, starting with surprise, and fixing her large black eyes upon me. On my bowing most respectfully, and repeating— "*Oui, Manselle, Madame*; I learn that by your husband's kindness, he is restored to the bosom of his family;" she, evidently much agitated, asked if my name was "*Boiçe*;" on my replying, "Yes, *Madame*, I am that unfortunate wanderer," she seized me by the hand, and immediately conducted me to the attics.

I happily succeeded in interesting her in my behalf, by so detailing my sufferings and disappointments, that she remained for some time immersed in tears, every now and then exclaiming, with genuine sensibility, "*Pauvre enfant; pauvre malheureux.*" Finding now, that I had gained another friend, whose influence with her husband was of some importance, I endeavoured to confirm her in the interest she felt for me, by holding forth the pecuniary advantages to be reaped from assisting us, and compared them with the attendant risk.

After some inquiries about Mansell, she left me to my reflec-

THE AUTHOR ENTERING THE GATE OF BRUGES PRECEDED BY MADAME DERIKRE

tions; and, although, from Moitier's having so frequently broken his word with Madam Derikre respecting us, I was not without apprehension, yet I was nevertheless determined, that something decisive should be the result of my trip.

At the expiration of half an hour, Moitier introduced himself, and commenced the conversation with relating difficulties innumerable. He represented the chance of detection in favouring the escape of prisoners, greater with him than any other person, as he was under the particular "surveillance" of the police; so much so, that his very footsteps were watched; and, that my presence in his house, if discovered, would be the cause of the confiscation of all his property; for which it was impossible I could make any adequate compensation.

Suspecting that these difficulties were only started to enhance the value of his intended services, and to draw from me an offer, I came immediately to the point, and proposed his putting us into some place of temporary security, under cover, until he could cause us to be landed in England; for which I offered him one hundred and fifty pounds, in bills, payable on demand.

He replied, that he had been put to considerable expense on account of Mansell, had not yet received a *stiver*, and had trusted solely to his honour; that if he now undertook this affair, and it failed, he should be ruined; however willing, therefore, he might be to serve us, he was necessarily obliged to decline having anything to do with it.

He questioned me about Mansell; when I endeavoured to convince him of the respectability of his connexions, and that his bills would be honoured, he appeared to waver; by this, I concluded, he had no objection to the undertaking, provided he was certain of payment; but, as I had no means of giving security, I endeavoured to excite his confidence, and proposed various plans; none of which seeming to please him, I requested he would leave me to myself for a few minutes, and I would, in the interim, turn over in my mind, other schemes; he consented, and left me. My object for requesting this suspension of the negotiation, was, to send him to his wife, whom, I had been informed by Madam Derikre, he always consulted upon any important matter, and as she had appeared disposed to be friendly towards me, it was a "ruse" I thought worth the experiment,

In about half an hour, Madam Moitier brought me up some coffee, gave me no hopes of her husband's assistance, but told me kindly, that I should remain there, till the evening. I thanked her, and again endeavoured to work upon her feelings, by dwelling upon our sufferings, and impressively representing the extreme distress to which we were reduced, by her husband's refusal to assist us.

She excused him, by pleading his poverty, and the risk of ruin; this I treated as very improbable, and enlarged with emphasis, on the paramount duty of an affectionate mother, to encourage her husband to, lay up in store for his children, and that to decline so favourable an opportunity as the present, was to do them an injury. To everything I said, she listened with apparent interest, and, promising to do all she could for me, retired.

Soon afterwards, Moitier came up, with "*bien faché, vraiment chagriné, même au desespoir.*" Until this moment I never doubted his intention to further our views, and had flattered myself, that, although he might not choose to take an open and active part, still he would prove the moving power, and that reaching his house in safety, would pave the way to final success; nevertheless, I persevered, as if I doubted not, and attributed our detention in this neighbourhood to the hopes his promises had created.

He assigned very cogent reasons for declining his aid, though he frankly admitted the proffered remuneration to be most liberal; but the dread of banishment from the district, as cutting off his professional resources, he being *Notaire publique*, seemed to outweigh the temptation. He, however, listened with intense interest to the recital of our adventures; when I seized the opportunity of appealing to his common sense, whether it was probable that officers, who had acted as we had done throughout, could be so base, so inconsistent, as finally to tarnish British integrity, by refusing to fulfil the very engagement which had probably saved our lives and restored us to our country.

Nevertheless, if it were more satisfactory to him, I added, I was willing that he should keep me as an hostage, and convey the other two to England; and when the money was paid, should procure me the means of following them. To this he objected, from the danger of concealing me in his house. I then proposed his placing me somewhere in the country, but he shrugged up his shoulders in reply, and paused in seeming doubt. I asked if he would have any objection to go to Verdun with bills which I would give him; he might there inquire who we were, get some of them cashed, and be insured payment for the remainder. At this, his countenance appeared to brighten, he consented to reconsider the matter, and retired.

About two hours had elapsed in this state of harassing uncertainty, when he came up again, and declared it was utterly impossible he could secrete three, but would not object to take me into his house, provided I had no intercourse with the others. At this proposal, a sudden glow of indignation flushed through my veins, which, for the moment, sealed my lips, and excited an inclination to turn my back upon him, and stalk out of the house; but, on reflection, I suspected it a mere *finesse*, to see if I was infamous enough to forsake my companions, and, therefore, with some warmth declared, that, however disastrous our continuing together might prove, it was my unalterable determination to share their fate,—with them to be restored to our country, or with them to be enchained in the dungeons of the enemy.

At length, despairing of bringing him to any decision, I requested the loan of a few *louis*, to enable us to purchase shoes and other necessaries for a long journey, as we intended to march through France and Germany to Trieste, and get home by the Mediterranean. For a moment he gazed with astonishment, and then exclaimed "*Mon Dieu! quelle persévérance.*"

After some further conversation, he desired me not hastily to depart, but to return to the woods, and there wait a few days; he would then be able to say positively whether he could assist us or not; at any rate, he would then lend us some money. As for that, I replied, with an air of indifference, he was as well able to lend us money now, as. he would be a week hence, and that, if he refused, I should, in the evening, join my comrades, and immediately proceed on our journey.

I saw that this kind of *hauteur* now became necessary; for it was evident his object was to gain time, in order to, ascertain the validity of Mansell's bills, and, satisfied on that head, he did not intend letting so good a speculation escape. I therefore requested, in a tone of firmness, a decided answer; this he declined, and left me.

Many reasons may be assigned for this man's conduct; but, it is probable, the prevailing one was, that he thought to make a greater profit by thus embarking us in detail. It was, however, sufficient to exonerate Mansell, in my mind, from any suspicion which might have existed, of his not having done all that he could for us; for every charitable allowance should be made for so inexperienced a youth being completely in the power of so experienced a rogue.

About two o'clock, Moitier returned, introducing Auguste Crens Neirinks. After some little preamble, it was agreed, that this Flemish "*Chevalier d'industrie*" should find us a place of concealment. Moitier was to go to Verdun, with my bills, to my friend Wills, [17] who, I knew, would risk his all to serve me; and, on his return, to hire, or purchase a boat for us. The success of my trip being thus complete, the next step was to communicate it to Whitehurst and Hunter, and get them into the town in safety.

Madam Derikre, whose anxiety to learn the result of the interview had detained her in a neighbouring public-house, was now despatched with these auspicious tidings. On her arrival at the "Cat," she sent her son into the woods, to escort its forlorn inmates through bye-paths and thickets so as to reach Bruges, just before the shutting of the gates, when mingling with the throng passing and repassing, they entered the town unobserved, and were conducted by her to the attics of a small uninhabited house, in a back street; here I rejoined them after dark.

---

17. Now Captain T. G. Wills, R. N.

The pleasure derived from success in any laudable undertaking, generally increases with reflection; and, in due proportion to the importance of the event. On this occasion, my delight was great indeed; and, if anything could heighten the enjoyment, it was the gratitude which my comrades expressed for bringing them to this place of security, and for the promising prospects that once more opened upon us, after a long career of anxiety and suffering.

In order to prevent any suspicion which might arise from intercourse with a house supposed to be uninhabited, a poor friend of the owner, was put in to occupy the front rooms. The furniture of our apartment, consisted of a table, four chairs, and a stump bedstead, filled with clean dry straw; this, compared to the sticks in the dirty wet *trou*, was a luxury only to be appreciated by those who have experienced similar vicissitudes.

During the absence of Moitier, Neirinks and his brother frequently visited us, and sent provisions by our fellow lodger. It was not until the 10th of April, that we were certain of Moitier's departure for Verdun. At this time, Neirinks introduced me to his family, consisting of an elderly mother, and her daughters, Mary and Pauline, with whom I frequently passed the evening, exciting the commiseration of these kind-hearted girls, by the relation of my adventures.

Moitier being now gone with despatches to Wills, and not likely to return for ten days, it occurred to me, that I might make an effort in the interval, to release Moyses, who, it will be recollected, was at Givet. Although, at first sight, the idea may appear a mere flight of the imagination, it led to such delightful reflections, and so much in harmony with my feelings towards him, that I indulged in them almost without intermission the whole day, and when Neirinks came in the evening, I mentioned it to him; but, finding he did not enter into the spirit of the enterprise, with a zeal promising success, I thought of going alone, and consulted Whitehurst and Hunter, in order the better to digest my plans; but they were averse to it, from friendship to me, and from the consideration of the numerous obstacles I should have to overcome.

There was, no doubt, truth and prudence in their observations; nevertheless, I resolved not to give it up. Accordingly, I again mentioned it to Neirinks, who, doubting how to act, yet desirous of gaining our confidence, now consented to assist me with the loan of his pocket book, together with certificates and passport; provided, that, in the event of my being taken, I would declare I had found them in a certain road.

This, however, was not all that was necessary, for money and clothes were wanting; at length, so many difficulties arose, that I feared success was impossible, still, as the plan I had laid down, though fraught with danger, afforded a chance, I felt that my friend was entitled to it; knowing, that if he were similarly situated, he would not hesitate a moment in risking his liberty, and even his life, to rescue me.

Indeed, so much was my mind occupied by these thoughts, and so much were my spirits exhilarated by this pleasing hope, that I worked myself into a belief, that an opportunity of proving my friendship now presented itself, in order to put its sincerity to the test. With this conviction, all hesitation vanished, and spurning impediments, I determined on the attempt, *coute qui coute*.

At length, Neirinks, seeing I was not to be diverted from the project, resolved to display a degree of *bravoure* on his *début* in this new speculation, and boldly consented to accompany me; as well as to furnish a little cash, clothes, &c. My plan was to proceed to Brussels, there to procure a *cabriolet*, and go on to Givet; leave them in the suburbs, and walk to the house of my old friend Lawmont, a surgeon in the navy, with my face bound up, under pretence of consulting him for the toothache; then smuggle a note into the prison to Moyses, desiring him to obtain leave to get into town, under pretence of marketing; and being escorted by an armed *gendarme*, he, of course, would not be on parole. Moyses was to endeavour to intoxicate, or in any way evade the guard, for which purpose he was to select one not averse to the juice of the grape.

It may be necessary to explain, that it was a common custom

in all the depôts of punishment, when any one of the rank of midshipman wished to go into town, to purchase provisions, or for other purposes, for him to be always accompanied by a gendarme, who expected his fee, the amount of which generally influenced him in the length of time he remained. Although this was supposed to be done in secret, it was always connived at by the commandant, who, probably, had his portion of it.

Succeeding thus far, Moyses was to get out of the town the best way he could, and join us in the suburbs; when we should immediately drive off for Brussels. At this place, a false passport was to be ready for him, to proceed and join the inhabitants of the garret. In the event of being pursued, we were to desert the *cabriolet*, fly to the woods, and travel to Bruges by night: or, if it should appear that Moyses could suggest any plan more practicable, I was ready to adopt it.

Neirinks having entrusted the secret of our intended enterprise to his sister Mary, a lass about eighteen, she sounded me on the subject, offering to go with us as far as Brussels, and there wait our return. I need not describe the astonishment this proposal excited, but it was not for me to question its propriety. I was, however, resolved her mother's consent should be first obtained, and I saw her for that purpose in the evening; it was then arranged, that we should travel as brother and sister, and Neirinks as a wine-merchant.

He gave me his pocket-book, and I studied his signature, which I could soon execute à *merveille* for, it may be proper to state, that in the examination of a traveller, when any doubt as to identity arises, he is ordered to sign his name, and it is compared with the one in the passport; if they correspond, the *gendarmes* seldom say more than "*cela suffit*," and he proceeds.

On the evening of the 14th of April, Neirinks, the young lady, and myself, in high spirits, took leave of our friends, and embarked in the night passage boat, by the canal, to Ghent; where we arrived the next morning, about nine, without meeting with any unpleasant occurrence. I took but little notice of my sister, there being several passengers in the boat who knew her. After our baggage was inspected, we took up our quarters in a tavern, in one of the squares, and sent our passports to the *municipalité*," to be examined, and countersigned.

Neirink having received orders from Moitier, to go to Antwerp and Flushing, to see if Peter the smuggler had returned from taking Mansell to England, I directed him to make himself acquainted with the state and number of the vessels of war, in those parts; also, with all the military strength in the neighbourhood; and he proved himself most discreet and indefatigable in obtaining this information.

After Neirink' departure, Mademoiselle and I amused ourselves by walking about the town, and visiting the fair. In this singular situation, I passed one of my pleasantest days during my stay on the continent.

To be accompanied and protected by an amiable and innocent little girl, rendered doubly engaging by the deep interest she manifested in my fate; to be thus escorted through a hostile town, where, if known, I should have been chained by the neck, and cast into its darkest dungeon; to be accosted with the appellation of *"frère,"* imperceptibly growing into *"mon cher frère;"* (*"Honi soit qui mal y pense"*)—was, indeed, an interesting novelty—a change of circumstances, which could not fail to excite the most lively feelings of gratitude and esteem, and which I shall ever think and speak of with the most pleasing recollections.

I felt myself bound to be particularly circumspect in my deportment. It was necessary to maintain a certain degree of easy vivacity, without being too forward; for this might have been considered as taking advantage of the confidence reposed in me; whilst being reserved would have appeared cold and insensible to the value of her protection.

In one of our promenades, during the two days we were at Ghent, we met about twenty prisoners, chained to each other by the neck, and escorted by four horse *gendarmes*; instead of turning down a cross street to avoid them, we walked boldly past, to the great amusement of my sister—of whose firmness of mind I cannot speak too highly.

Neirinks rejoined us on the third day with some important information, and assured us, that the vigilant manner in which the patrols performed their duty, communicating hourly, along the whole line of the coast, would render our embarkation extremely hazardous; this, however, was only a reason to be the more prudent.

On the 17th of April, we proceeded by the diligence to Brussels, where the same routine of sending our passports to the police-office was necessary to insure our safety. We escorted the lady to her aunt's, and retired to a public-house, where our conversation was generally upon the subject of wine, for fear of being overheard, knowing that such places swarmed with spies.

I went to the park, hoping to meet with an old Verdun acquaintance, named Hinds, residing here, through whom I expected to recruit my finances, and in whose friendship and secrecy confidence might be placed; but without finding him.

Neirinks and I then visited his aunt, to whom I was introduced as his brother "Jean," who had been absent many years; of this, however, the loquacious and merry old lady was not to be persuaded, and accused me of being the lover of her niece, for which, added she, you are the more welcome. Still passing by the name of "Jean," her daughter, if I mistake not, named Julie, an interesting young lady, about nineteen, received and embraced me as her long-lost cousin.

The next day, I again visited the, park, and, still missing Hinds, went to inquire at an adjoining hotel, when, to my surprise, I almost ran against a lieutenant of *gendarmerie*, standing at the door; I, however, strolled in, as if unconcerned, gently bending as I passed; but gaining no intelligence, I returned to the park, when, at length, meeting Hinds, and bowing respectfully.

I addressed him in French, for fear of observation. His surprise was so great, that he appeared to doubt the evidence of his senses; knowing, that five months before, I had broken out of a prison, only eighteen leagues distant.

We retired to his lodgings, where the leading occurrences

since my escape, and the cause of my visiting Brussels, were briefly related. He seemed to suspect a hoax, taxed me with having some deep scheme in view, which I would not disclose, cautioned me against remaining any time in the town, as the police was very strict, and assisted me with the loan of a few pounds.

On returning to Neirinks' aunt's, and entering the spacious drawing-room, I found the young ladies sitting *tête-à-tête* by a comfortable fire. As they arose when I drew near, I perceived a transparent drop trickling down the pale cheek of Julie, and something like confusion stealing over the evidently excited countenances of both; "*quel fatal prèsent du ciel, qu'un cœur sensible*"

Fearing that my untimely intrusion was the cause of this perturbation, I gently bowed, and was in the act of retiring, when Mary advanced, and modestly led me up to her cousin, who, with a graceful affability, presented her hand, faltering something quite unintelligible; nor could I divine the mystery of this scene, until she wished me a safe arrival in the bosom of my family. It being evident, by this observation, that she had been entrusted with the secret of my disguise, we drew very cosily round the fire, and I amused them with my history,

"Wherein I spoke of most disastrous chances,
"Of moving accidents by flood and field,
"Of hair-breadth 'scapes;"

which seemed to excite so lively an interest, that Julie entered into the spirit of the plot, with as much warmth and ardour as her cousin, and determined upon asking her mother's permission to return with us to Bruges; but it was not granted.

The next day, Neirinks not appearing, I strutted about the town, with the ladies under my arm; visited all the fashionable promenades, and, in the evening, went to the theatre: towards the close of the performance, Neirinks came in; we escorted the ladies home, and retired to our tavern.

On the 21st, under the responsibility of our jovial old aunt, we hired a *cabriolet*, left Brussels early for Charleroi, intending to take the cross road thence to Charlemont,[18] that being, as we thought, less dangerous. Nothing remarkable occurred, but the occasional meeting of a *gendarme*, which had now become so common an event, that it gave me little concern; still, however, I could not help feeling a degree of anxiety at the first sight of two of these fellows, standing at the door of a public-house in the village of Waterloo, where it was necessary that we should stop to bait the horse.

Neirinks proposed going on, but as he knew of no other house on the road, it might have created suspicion; I therefore judged it more prudent to brave it out, fully confident, should any question be asked, of cajoling them into the belief of our being wine-merchants.

We drove up to the door, jumped out, and called for the "*garçon d'écurie*," with an air of importance, in imitation of that French dignity, with which travellers are not unacquainted, gave the necessary orders, and mounted up the steps to the door, the two *gendarmes* opening, right and left, to make room.

In passing, I saluted them with "*Bonjour, Messieurs, peut on trouver à déjeûner ici;*" to which, reply was given in the affirmative; we walked in and ordered breakfast. Soon afterwards these fellows entered, and marched up, as if to question us; I forestalled them by an observation on the weather, and asking them if they had breakfasted, followed up this address with so rapid a succession of interrogatories and remarks, as to lead them into conversation, and prevent their being too inquisitive: when, proposing we should all breakfast together, they were so completely diverted from their apparent intention, that we sat down in a very friendly manner, and fared sumptuously, without any embarrassing inquiries.

Having paid the host, we continued our route, arrived at Charleroi, about seven in the evening, and supped with some countrymen, who informed us, the road to Charlemont was impassable for a *cabriolet* and that we should be obliged to go

---

18. Charlemont is a fortification situated on the left bank of the Meuse, commanding the two towns of Givet, whither we were bound.

round by Namur. After a savoury regale upon *fricandeau* and garlic, I retired to a comfortable bed; but my mind was so wholly engrossed by the pleasing reflections of meeting, and delivering my friend from bondage, that I could scarcely close my eyes.

The next morning, we set out for Namur, and arrived about noon. At three, we proceeded on our journey, intending to go no further that night than Dinant, about three leagues from Givet; so that the horse might be fresh on departing thence, with our prize. Just as we were approaching the southern gate, to our astonishment, and, I may add, confusion, we met Moitier, on his return from Verdun, who, no less surprised than ourselves at this unexpected *rencontre*, demanded where we were going, adding, without giving us time to reply—"Follow me," and went into an adjoining hotel.

On retiring into a private room, he gave me a letter from Wills, containing a confirmation of everything I had expected from so valuable a friend, and, indeed, more; for he had concealed and entertained Moitier at his house two days, treating him in the most handsome manner; got my bills cashed, and guaranteed payment of every engagement I should enter into with him. Strange to tell, Wills was the very first Englishman Moitier addressed on his arrival in Verdun.

The incredulous may probably smile at these extraordinary events, and term them "chance" but let him recall to mind the many such chances, herein recorded, and ask himself if they do not look like

"Chance, direction, which thou canst not see."

Moitier also told me that a brother mid named Blackwood had escaped from prison, and was secreted in Bruges, ready to join our party.

Wills's letter also gave me information of Moyses having been sent from Givet to Bitche, distant about two hundred miles, for an offence similar to the one for which I was *cachoted* in Valenciennes: but I had been so anxiously brooding over his anticipated rescue, that this letter did not, at first, destroy all hope of prosecuting my plans, even to the very walls of this horrible *bastille;* but, when I calmly discussed the subject with Moitier and Neirinks, the impracticability of success became so evident, that I was compelled, although very reluctantly, to abandon the design.

Moitier's vacillating, equivocal conduct, was now changed into a bold and steady determination to enter into the cause with spirit and energy: in proof of which, he offered to lend me any sum I chose to borrow. Leaving him to follow by the diligence, Neirinks and myself immediately departed for Brussels, but did not arrive until late that night.

Here we remained during the 23rd, not anxious to hurry back, knowing that we should be at Bruges before Moitier. This day was passed at "my aunt's"; the next, Neirinks, "my sister", and myself bade *adieu* to the family, and took the diligence to Ghent, where, on the following morning, we were joined by Moitier, who, in the afternoon, left us for Flushing, in order to make arrangements with Peter.

The next morning, we embarked in the canal-boat for Bruges, and arriving there after a pleasant day's journey, waited at the very public-house I had visited with my companions on the night of the 22nd of November, until (it being then after hours) the porter had taken our names to the commandant, with the request, that the gates might be opened—little could he imagine, that this application was, in part, made for an absconding English midshipman. After conducting "my sister" home, I rejoined my friends in the garret, who were much elated at my return; for, from my long absence, they were apprehensive I had been taken.

The relation of the various events which had occurred since our separation, afforded matter of amusement during the next day, though it was not without its alloy, arising from the failure of the expedition.

During my absence, Madam Derikre seeing the tattered state of my friends' wardrobe, applied to two Irish nuns in the convent, who in the spirit of true charity, discarding all religious prejudices, immediately sent them shirts, stockings, and a trifle in cash.

Soon after my return, I was introduced to a Mr. Edwards, an Englishman, residing in Bruges. I have since learnt, that it was this gentleman, who put Moitier in the right way of sending Mansell to England. Indeed, the imminent risk Mr. Edwards ran, in receiving Whitehurst and Hunter at his house, at all seasonable hours during my absence, to share his scanty meal, when they were literally starving, without even a hope of recompense, but that of our gratitude, and the pleasure derived from the performance of a benevolent act, cannot be mentioned without the warmest feelings of esteem.

In hourly expectation of Moitier's arrival from Flushing, with orders to depart, we waited till the 28th, when Neirinks brought word, that the guide would be in attendance the following day.

After my return, I passed the evenings with his family, and entertained his old mother with various tales, for by this time I had, with the aid of my fair friends, acquired sufficient knowledge of the Flemish language to make myself understood; the old lady could only speak her native tongue. From the account her daughter had given of our adventures, she evidently felt pleased with my attention.

I have already mentioned the agreement I had made with Moitier; but, on his return from Flushing, he declared that Peter, from the imminent risk he had run in his late trip, would not undertake to carry us across the Channel under 80*l*; that he, Moitier, had calculated on paying him only 40*l*: Peter was to receive one-half on landing in England, and a note of hand was to be left with Moitier for the other. The 80*l* were paid; but, I have since learned from Neirinks, that this story was a fabrication of Moitier's, who pocketed the additional 40*l*.

The hour of departure, from Bruges, now drawing near, I sent my *adieu* to Madam Derikre, repeating my assurance of the faithful discharge of her bills, which, with the cash she had already received, amounted to about 80*l*., besides what Mansell might have given her. To Madam Moitier also, I conveyed the expression of my best thanks, for all her attentions, assuring her, that although, in all probability, I should never see her again, yet, the recollection of the first reception I had met with from her, would ever excite my most heartfelt gratitude: and, that the manner in which her husband should be remunerated, would prove that she was not deceived, in the favourable opinion she had entertained of the honour of British officers.

On the 29th, soon after sunset, I visited Neirinks's family, expressed my acknowledgement of their kindness, more particularly to *"ma chère sœur,"* embraced them and departed.

Having rejoined my comrades, just at the close of the evening, we made ourselves as much like Flemings as possible, and stole out of the garret, singly, following each other at about fifty paces distance, conducted by Neirinks. Our almost only danger now was in not escaping the observation of the guard at the gates; but as, at this time, many people were passing and repassing, we mingled with the crowd, and, unnoticed, joined the guide, who was waiting in the vicinity.

Our joy was now great indeed, almost equal to that experienced when we found ourselves in the ditch, after descending the last rampart at Valenciennes. It had been previously arranged, that Neirinks should accompany us to England, to receive the stipulated reward.

Attended by him we marched in pairs, by woods and cross roads, towards the island of Cadsand, opposite to Flushing, till about one, a. m. expecting immediately to embark. On arriving near the coast, we met Peter's wife, who ordered us to lie down on the ground, whilst this Amazonian chief reconnoitred the strand. She had scarcely proceeded a hundred yards, when she was hailed, and saluted with a shot: like a skilful general, she instantly made good her retreat, and bivouacked with the main body.

In this position, we remained for about two hours, whilst Peter and his chief were occasionally watching the motions of the enemy, and looking out for the private signal from the boat. Our anxiety was now at its utmost stretch, and every passing moment appeared an age. The lookout, every now and then, was obliged to retreat, to avoid the patrols; although, had the boat arrived, being well armed, amidst irregular sand hills, and the spirits inflamed by confidence, our object could not have been defeated easily, or with impunity.

The boat not coming, when day dawned we retreated to Peter's hut, for concealment. This habitation in the midst of the sand hills had but one room; a few loose boards lying across from side to side upon mud walls, which supported a straw roof, formed a kind of ceiling to about one half of it: on these boards were spread some dry rushes, upon which we reposed. In this situation, day after day closed, whilst we expected each succeeding one to be the last in this country; but no appearance of the boat— and, as no exertions on our part could expedite its arrival, we did not quit the loft.

Peter finding the boat could not leave Holland so soon as he expected, and his hut being frequently visited by the custom-house officers, determined to advise our concealment in the subterranean passages of the ruins of the fortress of L'Ecluse.

On the very eve of our intended removal, the body of a youth, supposed to have been murdered, was there found; so that had we been taken in that situation, the presumptive evidence that we had committed the murder to prevent discovery would have been strong against us; this, coupled with our former offence of *chef de complot*, which no doubt would have been revived, in all probability would have subjected us to the punishment of death, or condemnation to the gallies; but Divine Providence, which had so repeatedly and so remarkably protected us throughout, here also interposed, and saved us from the threatened danger.

At length, on the 8th of May, positive information was brought, that all would be in readiness at ten p. m.; accordingly, at that hour, the weather fine, and the night dark, we marched down to the beach, and as soon as the patrol had passed, the private signal was made and answered. The boat gliding silently in shore with muffled oars; we rushed in with the rapidity of thought, and in an instant were all safe afloat; each seized an oar, and vigorously applying his utmost strength, we soon reached beyond the range of shot.

It were in vain to attempt a faithful description of our feelings at this momentous crisis; the lapse of a few minutes had wrought such a change of extremes, that I doubt, if amidst a confusion of senses, we could immediately divest ourselves of the apprehensions, which constant habit had engrafted on the mind; nor, indeed, could we relinquish the oar, but continued at this laborious, though now delightful, occupation, almost without intermission the whole night.

When day dawned, the breeze freshened from the eastward, and as the sun began to diffuse his cheering rays, the wide expanse of liberty opened around us, and in the distant rear—the afflicted land of misery and bondage, was beheld, with feelings of gratitude and triumph.

No other object intercepted the boundless prospect, save a solitary gun-brig, which was soon approached: naturally anxious to proceed with despatch, we passed on, and, unobserved, reached a considerable distance, when a boat was discovered making towards us; being in no fear of Frenchmen thus venturing so far from land, we hove to; and, having made the officer acquainted with the circumstances of our embarkation and destination, again spread the canvas, and made rapid progress to the N.W.

About noon, the wind still increasing, and the sea rising, it was deemed prudent to close reef the sail. While thus delightfully scudding before the foaming billows, which occasionally broke, as if to overwhelm our little boat, only fifteen feet in length, each eye was steadily fixed ahead, anxious to be the first to announce land. It was not, however, till towards three p. m. that the white cliffs were seen.

Although our situation was already replete with "joy and gladness;" still, the first sight of our native shore, after so long an absence, coupled with the recollection of conquered difficulties, excited increased happiness; and afforded ample compensation for past sufferings, though not without a pleasing hope, that promotion would be their reward.

On falling in with a fishing smack, at the back of the Goodwin Sands, the master welcomed us on board, and taking the boat in tow, ran for Ramsgate. On entering the harbour at five o'clock, I landed with such ineffable emotions of joy, and gratitude to that Almighty Disposer of events, who had vouchsafed to support and protect us through a constant succession of dangers and sufferings, during a period of nearly six months, and who, in his infinite mercy, had permitted our exertions to be finally crowned with success; that, with a heart throbbing almost to suffocation, regardless of the numerous spectators, I fell down, and kissed with rapture, the blessed land of liberty.

After a short conversation with the harbour-master, to our surprise and disappointment, we found that foreigners were not allowed to land here, but were ordered to Dover. Although convinced that they were in perfect safety, we felt it a point of honour not to have even the appearance of deserting those, to whom we were indebted for the happiness we now enjoyed: though the impatience to embrace our long-lost families (mine only eleven miles distant), may be more easily conceived than expressed.

We therefore determined to accompany, and see them comfortably placed in a public-house. To this end, I returned to the smack, the master of which agreed to run us down. Before making sail, I wrote a note to one of my brothers, residing at Margate, apprising him of my arrival, that he might communicate it to my family

We reached Dover about eight p. m., but not being permitted to land after dark, slept on board. At daylight, of the 10th of May, we landed, and having taken the foreigners to the Customhouse, thence to a public-house, and ordered them whatever they desired, we took chaises and departed for Betshanger, the residence of my father.

Mansell, on his return to England, anxious to bear glad tidings to my family, called at Betshanger, and, injudiciously, assured a younger sister, whom he happened to find alone, that "we should be either dead or in England in three weeks, as we had vowed not to be taken alive." Many months having elapsed since any letters from France had reached home, my parents received this information with mingled feelings of joy and fear, and immediately set on foot every method ingenuity and affection could devise, to render assistance through the smugglers.

As the time of the stipulated return drew to a close, so did parental fear and anxiety proportionally increase, till, at the expiration of six long weeks, hope itself sickened; still no returning child—no possibility of affording relief, nor of learning his fate; their minds agitated too with the consciousness, that if not already numbered with the dead, he must still be wandering through dreary woods, exposed to the severest sufferings, and "every man his foe." These were indeed heart-rending reflections, sufficient to harrow up the feelings, and tincture every thought with inconsolable grief. It was in the plenitude of these feelings, at the day's first dawn, for

"————Nature's soft nurse,
"Had fled their pillow:"

when they were endeavouring to afford mutual consolation, and actually discussing the propriety of family mourning, that my brother burst upon their deep, yet pious sorrow, with news of our safety and arrival.

The effect which this sudden information must have had upon the best of parents— parents alone can judge; suffice it to say, they were not unmindful that their prayers were heard by Him, "who is able to save."

On the road from Dover, at a moment when my attention was directed towards a neighbouring village, in search of the roof under which I had received the first impressions of discipline, Neirinks, whom I had taken with me, and who was admiring everything he saw, as *magnifique*, suddenly exclaimed—"*Regardez ce vénérable dans cette belle voiture,*" when I immediately recognized my father; we joined, and speedily drove to Betshanger, where a scene awaited me, that I had little anticipated.

But as I do not intend to intrude upon the public, what more properly belongs to private detail, let the imagination of the reader depict to himself this family meeting.

Nevertheless, as these pages may probably fall into the hands of some who may be desirous of knowing what became of the foreigners, and how we were all finally disposed of, I shall add, that Neirinks remained at Betshanger, until the return of the boat on the 17th, which, being put on board a gun-brig, was sent, together with the foreigners, off Flushing, by order of Commodore (now Admiral Sir Edward) Owen, to whom this little volume is dedicated as an offering of esteem.

With the money they received, and which they considered amply sufficient to recompense them for their services, they had previously purchased a quantity of indigo and coffee, which yielded them a profit of about 600 percent.

We had, therefore, not only the satisfaction of knowing that they were content with the result of their present trip, but that it would be an inducement for them to afford every assistance in their power to any of our countrymen, who might, at a future period, escape from confinement, and reach that part of the coast. Our own expenses amounted to 135*l* each.

Hunter was soon afterwards employed, and promoted in 1811. Whitehurst was sent to the Halifax station, where he had not been long before he was again made prisoner in the *Junon*, and detained in France during the remainder of the war. Mansell, a short time after, died at sea.

The day after my arrival I proceeded to London, and had the honour of an audience of Lord Mulgrave, then first Lord of the Admiralty. A few days subsequent to which, his lordship was pleased to issue an order for my examination, without waiting the usual period fixed for that purpose, and then immediately appointed me lieutenant of the *Arachne*.

This particular mark of his Lordship's approbation, in thus dispensing, in my favour, with the customary regulations observed on such occasions, was very flattering, and for which I was, in a great measure, indebted to Captain Sir Thomas Lavie, the senior officer of the prisoners of war, who, soon after our getting out of Valenciennes, had written to his lordship in my favour.

At the Admiralty, I learnt that Ricketts' father was in the *Theseus*, in the Downs. On my return into Kent, therefore, I apprised him of his son's situation, and of the obstacles which had prevented his accompanying me from Valenciennes, pledging myself that he would attempt escape, so soon as it could be done with credit to himself.

In June, Captain Sam. Chambers was appointed to command the *Arachne*, and when ready for sea, was ordered to Flushing.

The very first day I went on shore, in walking through Middleburg, I unexpectedly met my old friend, "Peter, the smuggler" who, to the amusement of some of our military officers, and my own temporary confusion, threw his arms round my neck, and kissed me.

Being in full uniform, I could at that moment, have dispensed with this public testimony of his joy, yet I was not so weak as to spurn it, or be insensible of its value:

"*à Rome comme à Rome.*"

I felt that I was still morally his debtor, for without him, I might, at that very hour, have been attired in a galley garb, decorated with a ponderous chain, far from this busy scene in lieu of the proud habiliment which thus innocently produced a transient blush.

Nevertheless, I was as much elated at the *rencontre*, as Peter could possibly be. But, reader, figure to yourself my increased delight, when, on retiring to an adjoining tavern, he put into my hand a letter from Ricketts, Rochfort, and Robinson, containing information of their having escaped from Valenciennes, and being then concealed in the neighbourhood of the "Cat."

As the *Theseus* was then at Flushing, not a moment was lost in communicating this joyful information to Ricketts' father, and in making preparations for the deliverance of the fugitives. In the meantime, the contents of the letter, through the channel of my worthy captain, were communicated to the commander-in-chief, together with my offer of services, who directed him to give me a written order to adopt such measures as I should judge prudent for their liberation.

This order was given to prove, in the event of my being made prisoner in the attempt, that I was no spy.[19]

In consequence of the capture of the island of Walcheren, which had taken place since my departure from this coast, it was reasonable to suppose that the vigilance of the enemy had considerably increased; it, therefore, became indispensably necessary, that the greatest circumspection should be observed in my proceedings.

On returning on board the *Theseus*, I found that the greater part of the ship's company had volunteered their services: thus evincing the eagerness with which every service of danger is courted by a well-organized ship's company. The crew of the eight-oared cutter (chosen for the occasion) claimed, however, the right of precedence, and to them was the task resigned.

Towards sunset, with this crew of *Bas Roads* "fire-eaters," for such were they designated on board, we made sail with a fresh and favourable breeze, accompanied by Peter.

On approaching the main, about midnight, we struck the mast, pulled in shore, with muffled oars, and landed him, unobserved by the patrols, on the very spot from whence I had embarked on the 8th of May. We rowed gently out, and came to a grapnel, about a musket-shot off, there we waited Peter's return with the fugitives, till dawn of day, when we returned to the Theseus without them.

After reporting my return to my captain, I went on shore

---

19. "H. M. Sloop *Arachne,* Flushing, *Sept. 20,*1809.
"Sir,
"Understanding there are several English persons, who have made their escape from the prison of Valenciennes, now in the neighbourhood of Bruges, and it meeting with the approbation of Sir Richard Strachan, K.B., &c, commander-in-chief, you are hereby directed to take such steps as you may think necessary for the liberation of the above-mentioned persons, taking care not to be absent more than twenty-four hours at any one time.
"I am, Sir, your humble servant,
"(Signed) Sam. Chambers,
"Comm. H. M. Sloop *Arachne.*
"To Lieut. Boys, H. M. Sloop *Arachne.*"

at Flushing, and there recognized a young Frenchman, named Ribierre a native of Verdun, who had been made prisoner at the capture of the island. At that time, my old friend, Captain Woodruff, was at the head of the transport department, in the expedition, I went to him to solicit his interest in behalf of Ribierre, when, with his accustomed benevolence, he immediately waited on the commander-in-chief, and obtained an order for his release; the night following, he was sent to France, but I never heard that he either thanked Captain Woodruff, or paid my friend, in Verdun, the money I lent him to take him home.

Five successive nights I returned with the crew of fire-eaters, and took up the position appointed by Peter, but no Peter was there.

On the sixth day, the *Arachne* was ordered to sea, and I was thereby most unwillingly deprived of the heartfelt satisfaction I had anticipated in being the deliverer of those very friends who had assisted in my escape from the citadel of Valenciennes. Happily, however, they did not suffer by my absence, for the same night my place was supplied by Lieutenant Edgar of the Theseus, who, although a stranger to the parties, nobly volunteered his services on the occasion. He proceeded to the same spot as before; about ten p.m. the private signal was made—he pulled in shore—in an instant Peter and the fugitives rushed into the boat, and were happily restored to their families and his Majesty's service.

Appendix

As there may be some readers desirous of knowing what transpired in Verdun after my departure, I have thought it necessary to add the following particulars.

In August, 1808, General Wirion found his system of "espionage" so very expensive, that he was compelled either to continue raising the necessary funds, or to abandon it in *toto*: to this, however, he could not yield; so that no sooner did one source of collection fail,' than he had recourse to others equally nefarious and degrading: thus he went on from exaction to exaction, until the representations of Sir Thomas Lavie to the Minister of War became so urgent, that Wirion was ordered to Paris to reply to the charges brought against him.

"His intimate friend Bernadotte (says Latreille, one of Wirion's minions), interested himself in his behalf with the Emperor, who answered, that he wished as much as any to draw Wirion out of the scrape, and that the best proof he could give of his inclination was to order his trial, and appoint him (Bernadotte) president of the Court. In September, 1809, so soon as this was announced to the unhappy general, he attired himself in full uniform, went to the Bois de Boulogne, and blew out his brains."

Such was the end of a man, who, with all his faults, possessed some good qualities, some transient moments, when he felt for the misfortunes of others, and revolted at the injustice he himself committed; the last fatal act of his existence proves, however much he may be condemned in a moral view, that he was not altogether lost to every sense of shame.

"It is the middle compound character which alone is vulnerable, the man who, without sufficient resolution to avoid a dishonourable action, has feeling enough to be ashamed of it."

The melancholy and ignominious death of Wirion made but a transient impression on his successor, the Colonel Commandant Courçelles, who, independently of a private fortune of a thousand a-year, was also commandant of the department of La Meuse, and, therefore, even penury could not be advanced in palliation of his turpitude.

On his first assuming the command, he was somewhat cautious, but he soon grew impatient of restraint and retail, and launched boldly out into wholesale plunder: to wit—he was possessed of extensive vineyards, and determined that the English should *"bon-gré mal-gré,"* assist in the consumption of their produce; to effect which, he had recourse to the Minister of War for an order to make the citadel a depôt of punishment. Pretences for arrest were soon found against nearly two hundred; when no wine was permitted to enter the gates but his own; and this was retailed at an exorbitant price, by his natural son, the jailor.

At length, Courçelles' extortions became so multiplied, and his conduct 90 tyrannical, that the midshipmen represented their many grievances to the Minister of War, amongst which was that of accusing him of pocketing the difference between the *franc* and the *livre-tournois* of their pay; which had amounted to £720.

Courçelles soon had intimation that what was passing in Verdun was known in Paris, which so alarmed him, that he sent for Massin, the lieutenant of *gendarmes*, and Curé, the paymaster; when, after several fruitless conferences, he persuaded the former to burn the accounts. Massin, deeply implicated in conscious guilt, seized the ledger, and threw it into the fire; thence arose a scuffle between the commandant, the lieutenant, and the paymaster; the two former endeavouring to destroy, the latter to preserve the book—the book, however, was burnt. The next day, the lieutenant, finding he had destroyed the only document which might have mitigated his offence, or pleaded some extenuation, by shewing that his superiors shared the spoil with him, retired to his quarters, and shot himself.

Courçelles was obliged to report this tragical event to the Minister of War, who, in reply, in September, 1811, summarily removed him from the command of the depôt, three days subsequently from that of the department, and final dismissal from the army, after a service of forty-six years.

Courçelles (as if to mark the extremes of evil and good) was succeeded in the command by Colonel the Baron de Beauchene, who immediately renounced all secret police, spies, and informers; broke up the establishment in the citadel; restored all to parole; and granted permission to many to reside in the country; in a word, he conducted the depôt in such a mild, gentlemanly manner, that he was revered as a father, rather than a military keeper of a numerous assemblage of prisoners of war; the effect of which was an immediate stop to desertion, which during Courçelles' reign had averaged nearly one a-week,

A new measure was adopted, which would have had a beneficial effect during the Wirion or Courçelles' administrations, namely, that which was termed a Council of Administration. This consisted of three French and two English officers, for the purpose of inquiring into all complaints; but under the Baron de Beauchene, who was the very fountain of justice and equity, it proved of very little use.

The career of this great and good man, who united every social virtue with the lofty feeling of the veteran soldier, was unfortunately but too short, he was taken ill on the 21st of March, 1813, and died on the 27th, respected and lamented by everyone. Nearly the whole body of the English, attired in full uniform or deep mourning, attended the funeral: thus shewing that it matters not in what country a good man is born, for reason (with the reasonable) will dispel all prejudice and constrain even his enemies to venerate his virtues and his memory,

The prisoners immediately set on foot a subscription for the erection of a monument, little suspecting, that the jealousy and hatred of the French government to the English, would frustrate a design which would have proved a proud memorial of the pre-eminent virtues of the individual, and a lasting encomium on the magnanimity of both nations.

On the death of De Beauchene, General Dumolard succeeded to the government of the depot; but one short month was sufficient to prove that the Courçelles' tyranny was not to be renewed with impunity, and he was superseded towards the latter end of April, by Major de Meulan.

This gallant soldier, as honourable as brave; as generous as just; adopted the mild measures of the high-minded De Beauchene, and thus continued to alleviate misery and diffuse contentment and resignation to the care-worn captive, until the French armies, meeting with serious reverses, rekindled a hope of deliverance, that had been nearly extinct for ten long years. At length the glorious battle of Leipsic was fought, which compelled the French armies to retreat to the Rhine.

In January, 1814, soon after the allied armies had crossed the Rhine, the depôt was ordered to be removed to Blois, in the department of Loire and Cher. During the three days, given for the accomplishment of this order, scenes of confusion occurred never before witnessed in Verdun. Eleven hundred prisoners of all ranks, rejoicing and exulting in the move; of whom one hundred had families; two hundred, from age and infirmity, together with five hundred children, needing carriages, and few horses to be procured.

About three hundred young women claiming, by the ties of affection, the right of emigration; tumultuous assemblages in almost every street; Jews and tradesmen bustling from house to house for payment of debts, when by far the greater number of prisoners were almost penniless. The military chest exhausted, and unreplenishable from the rapidly approaching theatre of war. Major de Meulan gone to Blois;—thence no commanding officer; no arrangements; no subordination; and the feeble French authorities in hourly dread of the English taking possession of the place. These conflicting occurrences combined to give Verdun, during these three days, the appearance of a modern Babylon.

Vehicles and draught quadrupeds of every description were put in requisition, and congregated masses of youth and age, of vigour and infirmity, moved off in dense confusion, affording a faint idea of Israel's retreat from the land of Egypt.

Scarcely had the prisoners been a fortnight at Blois, when the rapid approach of the allies upon Orleans, compelled a further removal of the depôt to Gueret, in the department of La Greuse, when the prisoners experienced sad distresses, which would have been seriously aggravated but for the mild and judicious arrangements of Major de Meulan.

It was computed that there were about 21,500 English at that time in France, *viz*.

Verdun	1100
Sarre Louis	3000
Givet	2500
Arras	3000
Valenciennes	2000
Longuy	1500
Briançon	3000
Mont Dauphin	1000
Bitche	400
Cambray	2000
Sedan	500
Auxonne	1500
	21,500

All the depôts in the eastern departments were put in motion about the same time as that of Verdun. It was said that had there been a single individual in each of these, capable of directing the movements of large bodies of men, they might easily have taken possession of these places, and joined the allies. But this was incorrect; for the men grown grey in the tedious monotony of a prison, had so completely lost all energy, save that of mere animal existence, that they may be said to have become not only indifferent to change, but actually attached to their cells—so much are we the children of habit. Thus they were marched, in large masses, from prison to prison, with scarcely an individual effort made for liberty.

The Verdun division, on parole at Gueret, did not long continue there, for on the 2nd of April, 1814, news arrived of the abdication of Buonaparte, when they were all set at liberty. The other depôts also marched for the coast, and embarked for England; many of them after a cruel, wanton, barbarous, and unprincipled imprisonment of nearly eleven years.

ALSO FROM LEONAUR
AVAILABLE IN SOFTCOVER OR HARDCOVER WITH DUST JACKET

CAPTAIN OF THE 95th (Rifles) *by Jonathan Leach*—An officer of Wellington's Sharpshooters during the Peninsular, South of France and Waterloo Campaigns of the Napoleonic Wars.

BUGLER AND OFFICER OF THE RIFLES *by William Green & Harry Smith* With the 95th (Rifles) during the Peninsular & Waterloo Campaigns of the Napoleonic Wars

BAYONETS, BUGLES AND BONNETS *by James 'Thomas' Todd*—Experiences of hard soldiering with the 71st Foot - the Highland Light Infantry - through many battles of the Napoleonic wars including the Peninsular & Waterloo Campaigns

THE ADVENTURES OF A LIGHT DRAGOON *by George Farmer & G.R. Gleig*—A cavalryman during the Peninsular & Waterloo Campaigns, in captivity & at the siege of Bhurtpore, India

THE COMPLEAT RIFLEMAN HARRIS *by Benjamin Harris as told to & transcribed by Captain Henry Curling*—The adventures of a soldier of the 95th (Rifles) during the Peninsular Campaign of the Napoleonic Wars

WITH WELLINGTON'S LIGHT CAVALRY *by William Tomkinson*—The Experiences of an officer of the 16th Light Dragoons in the Peninsular and Waterloo campaigns of the Napoleonic Wars.

SURTEES OF THE RIFLES *by William Surtees*—A Soldier of the 95th (Rifles) in the Peninsular campaign of the Napoleonic Wars.

ENSIGN BELL IN THE PENINSULAR WAR *by George Bell*—The Experiences of a young British Soldier of the 34th Regiment 'The Cumberland Gentlemen' in the Napoleonic wars.

WITH THE LIGHT DIVISION *by John H. Cooke*—The Experiences of an Officer of the 43rd Light Infantry in the Peninsula and South of France During the Napoleonic Wars

NAPOLEON'S IMPERIAL GUARD: FROM MARENGO TO WATERLOO *by J. T. Headley*—This is the story of Napoleon's Imperial Guard from the bearskin caps of the grenadiers to the flamboyance of their mounted chasseurs, their principal characters and the men who commanded them.

BATTLES & SIEGES OF THE PENINSULAR WAR *by W. H. Fitchett*—Corunna, Busaco, Albuera, Ciudad Rodrigo, Badajos, Salamanca, San Sebastian & Others

AVAILABLE ONLINE AT **www.leonaur.com**
AND OTHER GOOD BOOK STORES

NAP-1

www.ingramcontent.com/pod-product-compliance
Lightning Source LLC
Chambersburg PA
CBHW021005090426
42738CB00007B/655